CHARLINE

GOOD COOKING

always!!

- Paul

-87

For
Mildred and Mildred

FIREMAN CHEF JIM NEIL'S FAVORITE RECIPES VOLUME II

Written by
Jim Neil
and
Mary Petersen Neil

Illustrated
by
Joseph Blake

Cover Photography by
Michael Jang

CONTENTS

ISBN 0-9618761-0-7

PUBLISHED BY
PJ Books
P.O. Box 23803
Oakland, California 94623

Designed and printed by
Kroma International Graphics Center, Inc.
Spokane, WA, USA

ACKNOWLEDGEMENTS

A very special thank you to these friends who have given us their time, support, encouragement and understanding to make this dream come true: Ann Fraser, Ross McGowan, De Anne Hamilton, Karen Stevenson, Barbara Lane, Mary Windishar, Ron Lorentzen, Victoria Ruiz, Hank and Dodie Moore, Caryl Saunders, Steve Giraudo, Ray Yim, the technical and production staffs of KPIX, the men at Station "2", S.F.F.D. for being honest critics, Bill Tribolet for his wine contributions, Mom Neil and Mom Petersen for their many hours in the mailroom, Jennifer Ann for her computer assistance, Pat McEvoy for his editing and "the typist" for her incredible patience, motivation and sincere belief in our dreams.

JIM and MARY

FORWARD

''Fireman Chef'' Jim Neil has continued to delight his audiences on the KPIX ''People Are Talking'' show in San Francisco, California. Currently in his seventh year on the show, Jim is now getting requests for his recipes by the thousands each week. In response to many of the viewers, he and Mary have written this second cookbook which is a collection of the recipes Jim featured during his second three years on the show.

A review of this volume has shown me again that he still remains very simple and practical in his approach and without undue duplication adds a flare for the more creative individual. The recipes are unique, economical, fun and still remain within the ''family'' influence. A favorite of mine is the ''Minced Cornish Game Hens with Apricot Stuffing''. I have personally delighted some very critical palates with the finished product.

Besides a firefighter, chef and husband, there is another facet of Jim's life with Mary that I should mention....their support and devotion to community projects. They give countless hours to Laguna Honda, a Hospital in San Francisco where multiple sclerosis patients are hospitalized; they host the cooking demonstrations at the annual ''Festa Italiana''; they support the March of Dimes at the annual telethon and the ''Gourmet Gala''; they work on committees with the San Francisco Professional Food Society; they're involved with the Garlic Festival, the Zucchini Festival....the list goes on and on. Each is happy to take time from their individual careers to help others. I am proud to be a brother and a friend.

The variety of recipes that you will find in this Volume II is extraordinary. An entire menu can easily and economically be prepared with most enjoyable results. May you continue to share your enthusiasm and dedication to the culinary arts, as I have, with this cookbook.

CHEF ROBERT F. NEIL
Retired

INTRODUCTION

It doesn't seem like it has been three years since we wrote our first cookbook. It has been a fun and exciting time for us .... we are now "Mr. and Mrs. Jim Neil", we have purchased a new home (complete with a cat), and we have written our second cookbook.

The comments have been very positive about Volume I, so when Volume II became a reality we kept the same format. It is a collection of about 150 recipes which Jim featured his second three years on the show; it has the large, easy to read print and there is one recipe per page.

The basic concept of Jim's segments on "People Are Talking" is the same; he likes to prepare recipes that are easy, delicious, and economical,with ingredients that are available at the local supermarket. There is, however, a new feature that has been added to the show, "Jim's Picks". Once a month Jim visits a restaurant in the Bay area, meets with the chef, discusses a "specialty" of the restaurant, and then prepares the recipe on the show. It is not a restaurant review; it is Jim's way of exposing his viewing audience to a restaurant he feels is worth their consideration when dining out. You will find these recipes listed in the index under "Jim's Picks."

Jim's interest in cooking is continually expanding, although he never loses the basics he learned in cooking school. He tries new recipes almost daily, either at home or at the firehouse. He knows if he gets the "okay" from the guys at Station #2, it will be popular with his viewing audience.

We have been pleased with the overwhelming response we have received from Volume I and know that you will be doubly excited and pleased with what Volume II has to offer.

Enjoy and good cooking always!!!

Jim & Mary Neil

Photo by Michael Jang

Photo by Elizabeth Knefel

Jim Neil and Ann Fraser with guest chef Jeremiah Tower. See recipe for "My Aunt's Cole Slaw" page 74.

Photo by Darcy Provo

Jim Neil with Rita Channon and Jan Yanehiro from Evening Magazine at a March of Dimes fund raising dinner. See recipe for "Crab Cakes" page 2.

Photo by Elizabeth Knefel

Ross McGowan, Ann Fraser and Jim Neil with guest chef Paul Prudhomme. See recipe for "Sauteed Crawfish" page 158.

Photo by Darcy Provo

Ann Fraser and Jim Neil with guest chef Laurie Burrows Grad preparing "Double Fudge Chip Cake", see recipe on page 230.

APPETIZERS

Crab Cakes
Fish Mousse
Eggplant Sandwiches
Artichoke Spread
Rumaki
Sweet and Sour Meatballs
Party Mix
Walnut Spread
Mushrooms Stuffed with Crabmeat
Shrimp Mousse

Crab Cakes

Each year I enjoy being involved with the Gourmet Gala, a local fundraiser for the March of Dimes. In 1985, working with Jan Yanehiro and Rita Channon, of "Evening Magazine," we prepared these award-winning crab cakes. (See photo, page xii)

1 Cup crab meat
½ Cup bay shrimp, chopped
1 Egg, slightly beaten
½ Cup bread crumbs, unseasoned
1 Tablespoon shallots, chopped
¼ Cup parsley, freshly chopped
¼ Cup Jack cheese, finely grated
1 Cup mayonnaise
1 Garlic clove, minced
Freshly ground pepper, to taste
Dash Worcestershire sauce

Combine all ingredients. Mix well and form into patties approximately 2 inches in diameter. Pat on additional bread crumbs. Fry in butter or oil, over medium high heat, for approximately 1-2 minutes on each side, or until golden brown. Garnish with fresh parsley and serve immediately with tomato pepper mayonnaise (page 61).

Fish Mousse

I enjoy fish as a main course, but I also think it makes a marvelous light first course. This mousse may be served warm or cold. I like to serve it with a nice garlic mayonnaise (see Tomato-Pepper Mayonnaise on page 61) and a glass of chilled Sauvignon Blanc.

1 Pound white fish filets (sole, bass or rock cod)
¼ Pound smoked salmon (4 slices)
2 Eggs
8 Tablespoons butter, unsalted
2 Cups heavy cream
Salt and pepper, to taste
Parsley sprigs

Wash and dry fish filets. Check for bones. If there are some, remove with pliers. Put fish filets and eggs into food processor. Puree until smooth. Remove to a bowl. Without cleaning the processor, cream the butter. With processor still running, add the fish mixture, a little bit at a time. Salt and pepper, to taste. Add the cream slowly, until a smooth consistency is reached.

In a well-buttered loaf pan, lay 2 slices of the smoked salmon on the bottom. Spoon in ½ of the pureed fish mixture. Layer with the other 2 slices of salmon. Spoon in the remaining mixture. Cover loosely with a buttered piece of foil or parchment. Place in a water bath (cake pan ½ full of warm water). Bake in a 350° oven for 45 minutes. When cool, invert onto a serving platter. Slice into individual servings and garnish with sprigs of fresh parsley.

Eggplant Sandwiches

Carlo Middione is a great Italian chef with a wonderful wit and keen sense of humor. He was my guest on the "People Are Talking" show in May, 1984. We prepared "Fetti di Melanzane Ripieni" or Eggplant Sandwiches. They are a delicious appetizer which may be served hot or cold. A glass of nicely chilled Italian dry white wine would be a perfect compliment.

Choose a firm, shiny eggplant with tight skin and no blemishes. If eggplant is more mature, salt slices lightly and let drain in a colander for an hour. Pat dry with paper towels.If flesh is cream colored and seeds are not easily visible, there will be no need to salt the eggplant to draw out the bitter juices.

Jim's Featured Pick:

VIVANDE PORTO VIA
2125 Fillmore Street
San Francisco, CA
(415) 346-4430

1 Eggplant, approximately 1¼ pounds
Thinly sliced mortadella
Thinly sliced provolone cheese
2 Eggs, beaten
⅓ Cup fine dry breadcrumbs, unseasoned
⅓ Cup Parmesan cheese, freshly grated
2 Tablespoons minced Italian parsley (optional)
Olive oil

Slice eggplant crosswise into 12 or 14 circles of equal thickness. Tear mortadella to fit in a single layer between two slices of eggplant. Fold provolone similarly and place over mortadella on each of the 6 or 7 "sandwiches." Press down on each sandwich so filling will cling to eggplant. Dip sandwiches first in beaten egg, coating evenly and well. Then dip into the plate of bread crumbs, Parmesan cheese and parsley. Be sure to coat edges as well as tops and bottoms with crumb mixture. Drizzle ½ teaspoon of good Italian olive oil over each sandwich, top and bottom. Arrange on a baking sheet and place in a preheated 375° oven for approximately 30 minutes or until golden brown and crisp. Let set 5-10 minutes before cutting into wedges to serve.

I think an appetizer before a meal should stimulate the palate so I rarely offer more than one selection and I prepare a limited amount as I want my guests to enjoy the dinner.

Each of these Appetizers can be prepared in advance and baked at the last minute as they're best if served warm.

Artichoke Spread

2 Cups artichoke hearts, water packed, drained
2 Cups mayonnaise
2 Cups Parmesan cheese, grated

Chop artichoke hearts in food processor. Add mayonnaise and cheese. Blend well. Pour into a baking dish and place in a preheated 350° oven. Bake for 20-25 minutes or until the mixture bubbles. Serve immediately with crackers or sliced baguettes.

Rumaki

12 Chicken livers
1 Can water chestnuts (drained)
1 Pound sliced bacon

Quarter each liver. Slice the water chestnuts. Wrap a piece of liver and water chestnut in a slice of bacon. Secure with a toothpick and place under a preheated broiler until the bacon is crisp. Serve immediately.

Sweet and Sour Meatballs

1 Pound ground beef
1/4 Cup water
1/4 Cup breadcrumbs
1 Egg
1 Small onion, grated
1 Teaspoon salt
1/8 Teaspoon pepper, freshly ground
1 Cup canned chili (without beans)
1/2 Cup grape jelly
Juice of one lemon

Combine ground beef, water, breadcrumbs, egg, onion, salt and pepper. Blend well. Shape into 1 inch meatballs. Place on a greased baking pan. Bake in a 350° oven for 20 minutes. Meanwhile, combine chili, grape jelly and lemon juice in a medium saucepan. Mix well. Simmer. When the meatballs are done, remove from oven. Add to sauce. Stir gently. Simmer about 1 hour, stirring occasionally. Serve warm.

When Mary and I entertain in our home, we usually have two or three couples over for an evening of dining. Occasionally, however, we like to give a large party, with a lot of friends, and serve a variety of appetizers. These recipes are perfect for a crowd!

Party Mix

1 Box Cracklin Bran cereal
½ Box Veri Thin pretzel sticks
2 8 ounce packages corn nuts
1 24 ounce jar unsalted dry roasted peanuts
1 6 ounce can hickory smoked almonds
2 16 ounce cans mixed nuts
2 12 ounce jars dry roasted cashews

Place everything in a large bowl. Mix well. Store in an airtight container until you are ready to serve.

Walnut Spread

½ Cup butter
½ Cup bleu or roquefort cheese
3 Tablespoons cognac or bourbon
¼ Cup walnuts, finely chopped

Combine butter, cheese and brandy in food processor until smooth. Stir in walnuts. Allow to rest at least 2 hours or overnight. Serve with pumpernickel, raisin bread, crackers, or fresh assorted vegetables.

Mushrooms Stuffed with Crabmeat

2 Tablespoons butter
1/4 Cup green onions, finely chopped
3 Tablespoons flour
1 Cup milk
1/4 Teaspoon salt
1/8 Teaspoon cayenne pepper
1/2 Teaspoon lemon juice, freshly squeezed
12 Ounces crabmeat
24 2 inch mushroom caps
Salt and pepper, to taste
1/2 Cup fresh bread crumbs, unseasoned
2 Tablespoons parsley, freshly chopped

In a sauce pan, melt butter. Add onions and saute 2 minutes. Stir in the flour and cook for an additional 2 minutes. Whisk in milk and bring to a boil. Reduce heat to simmer and cook 3-5 minutes or until the sauce is thick enough to coat a spoon. Season with salt, cayenne pepper and lemon juice. Set aside. Flake crabmeat into a medium sized bowl. Stir the sauce into the crabmeat. Clean mushroom caps. Sprinkle lightly with salt and pepper. Fill with crabmeat mixture. Top with bread crumbs. Bake in a 350° oven for 20 minutes. Remove from oven. Let set for 7-10 minutes. Sprinkle with chopped parsley. Serve on a heated platter.

Shrimp Mousse

While traveling on a short vacation to Seattle, Mary and I stayed at the downtown Sheraton. On Sundays, high atop the hotel, they offer a special buffet brunch. It is an incredible assortment of fresh seafood from the Northwest. Displayed are salmon, halibut, prawns, oysters, clams and squid. As a first course, everyone is presented a small portion of a warm shrimp mousse, warm dill rounds and a glass of champagne. We enjoyed it so much that when we got home, we created our own shrimp mousse.

Garnished with sprigs of fresh dill, it is a beautiful and elegant first course at a dinner party or for a larger crowd, a marvelous appetizer!

P.S. If you are ever visiting Seattle, a "must" is to spend a day walking through the "Pike Place Market."

¼ Pound fresh prawns, peeled and deveined
1 Small garlic clove
2 Tablespoons butter, unsalted
2 Eggs
4 Teaspoons whipping cream
1 Tablespoon dry sherry
Salt and pepper, to taste
¼ Teaspoon dried dill

Place all ingredients in food processor and blend. Spoon into a one quart baking dish. Sprinkle with additional dill. Place in a water bath (cake pan ½ full of warm water). Bake in a 350° oven for 30 minutes. Serve warm or cool with toasted dill rounds.

Toasted Dill Rounds

1 Cube butter
2 Tablespoons fresh dill, chopped (or 1 tablespoon dried)
1 Baguette

Place butter and dill in food processor. Blend well. Cut baguette into ¼" slices. Butter each slice and arrange on a cookie sheet. Place under broiler for 1-2 minutes or until bread is toasted. May be served warm or at room temperature.

TRUCK
2
SFFD

SOUPS

Bat Stew
Bean Soup
Clam Chowder
Crab Chowder
Cream of Artichoke Soup
Creamy Crab and Avocado Soup
Curried Carrot Soup with Chives
Gazpacho
Irish Stew
Thai Sour Shrimp Soup
Vegetable Soup

Bat Stew

My guest chef, Joanie Greggains, "Fitness Expert," has been a regular on the "People Are Talking" show since 1978. Her segments on Monday mornings are informative and entertaining covering such topics as nutrition, health and exercise.

In 1979, Joanie created "Morning Stretch" which became a KPIX series and subsequently went into national syndication. Today the series is seen daily in over 110 cities with an audience of over 100 million. In addition to being the star and executive producer of "Morning Stretch," Joanie is a best selling author and producer of record albums, videos and a series of exercise cassettes. She is truly one of America's top experts on physical fitness.

Joanie says that the recipe is so named "Bat Stew" because of the light brown color of the mushrooms when they are cooked. She also demonstrated how to slice the mushrooms and cut notches to resemble the silhouette of a flying bat.

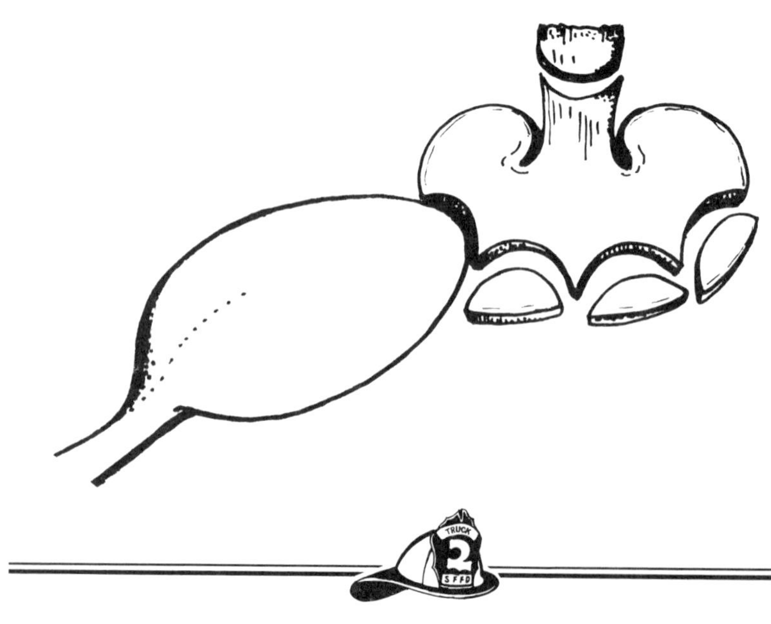

1 Large onion
½ Pound mushrooms, thickly sliced
1 Cup ricotta cheese
1 Tomato, chopped
1 Cup baby green peas, (fresh or frozen)

Put a small amount of vegetable oil in a saucepan and saute onions and mushrooms until soft. Add ricotta, tomato and green peas. Stir until warmed through. Serve at once.

Bean Soup

Dried beans are inexpensive and very nutritious. There are many varieties of dried beans on the market. When I refer to white beans in the recipe, you can use either Great Northern or Navy beans. The great northerns will take about 15 minutes longer to cook than the smaller white navy beans. One cup of white beans will produce about four cups of cooked beans. To preserve some of the food value, use some of the soaking liquid in the cooking process.

I always start a day or two in advance when I make this soup. I soak my beans overnight and cook my ham hocks or shanks the day before. The ham imparts a wonderful flavor into this very hearty soup stock. If the stock is too salty, add about one half of the bean liquid. Sometimes when good Swiss chard is not available, I will substitute cabbage.

2 Pounds white beans
Leftover ham bone or 4 ham shanks or hocks
2 Onions, chopped
12 Carrots, sliced
2 Bunches Swiss chard, rinsed and chopped

Place beans in a pot and cover with cold water. Let set overnight, uncovered. A quick method is to bring beans to a boil for one minute, then remove from heat and let set for one hour, uncovered.

Cover ham bones or shanks with six quarts of cold water. Bring to a boil, skimming any foam as it rises to the top. Reduce heat to a simmer for two to three hours, uncovered. Remove bones and trim off any meat, discarding any fat. Return meat pieces to pot. Cool two to three hours and then refrigerate several hours or overnight. When fat has hardened, skim off and discard. This mixture should yield about four quarts of stock. When ready to use, return to stove and heat. Add onions and beans. Cook beans until tender, about one hour. Add carrots and Swiss chard. Continue cooking until carrots are tender, 20-30 minutes. This will keep in the refrigerator, covered, up to one week and freezes very well. Yield: 4 quarts soup.

Clam Chowder

Nothing is more exhilerating on a clear day than a walk along the beach watching the ocean. Maybe it's the fresh salt air or the sand under your feet that whets the appetite. It's then that Mary and I head to the "Cape Cod on the California Coast" for a bowl of their famous clam chowder.

It has always been argued as to which chowder is the best, the red or the white. I like both as I love clams. If you have fresh clams available, use them; they will add greatly to the flavor.

This white chowder, from the "Shore Bird" is rich and creamy. The chef usually makes a batch of 30-40 gallons at a time and leaves it set for a day to help enhance the flavor. He uses coarsely chopped, not minced, clams. The fish bouillon cubes are available at your local supermarket in the soup section.

Jim's Featured Pick:

THE SHORE BIRD
390 Capistrano Road
Princeton-By-The-Sea, CA
(415) 728-5541

3 Ounces bacon, diced
2 Small potatoes, diced
1 Cup celery, diced
1 Small onion, diced
12 Ounces chopped clams
3 Cups clam juice
1 Fish bouillon cube
1 Ounce lemon juice
1 Tablespoon basil
1 Tablespoon thyme
Tabasco, to taste
Freshly ground white pepper, to taste
4 Tablespoons butter
4 Tablespoons flour
2 Ounces cream cheese
3 Cups milk

Saute the bacon, celery and onion in a heavy sauce pan. Boil potatoes in a separate pot, until tender, yet firm. Add clams, clam juice, bouillon cube, lemon juice, basil, thyme, tabasco, pepper and cooked potatoes to bacon/celery/onion mixture. Simmer. In a small sauce pan, blend butter and flour. Cook for a minimum of 8-10 minutes, stirring constantly. Add flour mixture to clam mixture and gently stir in cream cheese. Add milk and warm until heated through. Serve.

Creamy Crab and Avocado Soup

Every February, Pier 39 in San Francisco sponsors a Crab Festival as a fund-raiser for the March of Dimes. The event usually includes a crab recipe contest, several cooking demonstrations by Bay Area chefs and an "All You Can Eat" crab dinner. It is a fun, worthwhile event.

I always jump at the chance to help judge the recipe contest because of my love for crab. This is the recipe we awarded first place when I judged the 1985 cookoff held at "Neptune's Restaurant" on the Pier. It was prepared by Mrs. A. Cohn of Napa, California.

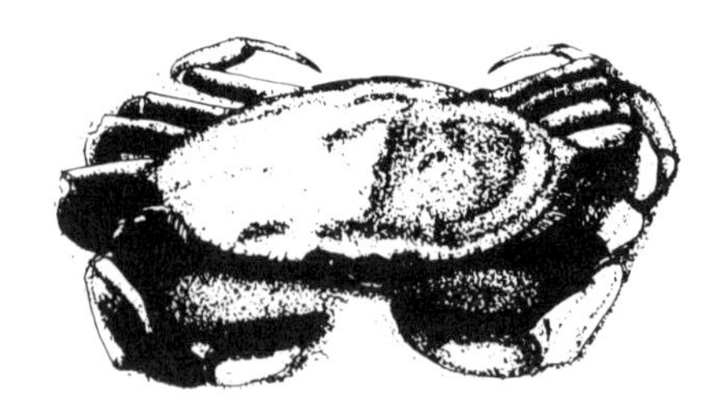

1 Tablespoon oil
2 Tablespoons butter
1 Medium onion, chopped
1 Garlic clove, chopped
1 Stalk celery, diced
1 Cup dry white wine
2 Cups mild fish stock
½ Teaspoon tabasco sauce
1 Whole Dungeness crab, cooked and cleaned
1 Cup heavy cream
2 Ripe avocados
1 Cup sour cream
1 Small ripe tomato, peeled, seeded and chopped
Salt, to taste

Melt butter with the oil in a sauce pan over low heat. Add the onion, garlic and celery. Saute 10 minutes on low heat. Add the wine and simmer an additional 10 minutes. Add the fish stock and continue cooking for 10 minutes. Remove from heat. Stir in salt, tabasco sauce and crab meat. Puree mixture in a blender or food processor. Peel one of the avocados and remove the pit. Cut into several pieces. Puree avocado and heavy cream together. Stir this mixture into the crab mixture. Cover. Chill 3 hours or overnight. To serve: peel remaining avocado and cut into 12 slices. Seed, core and chop tomato. Place 2 slices of avocado on top of each serving of soup, so they resemble a heart. Spoon 1 tablespoon of sour cream into the center of each heart and garnish with 1 teaspoon of chopped tomato on the sour cream. Serves: 6.

Cream of Artichoke Soup

The artichoke industry began in Castroville, California, back in 1922 with only a few acres of plants. Today there are more than 12,000 acres in four counties on the central California coast where artichokes are grown. The plants grow as high as four feet with a diameter of six feet. They look very similar to a great fern and produce a beautiful violet-purple flower when the bud is left on the stalk.

Although artichokes are harvested the year around, the peak season is March, April and May, with a lesser season in the fall. Artichokes are planted, cultivated and harvested by hand. When selecting artichokes, look for the brightest, greenest globes you can find.

Artichokes are low in calories, usually 50 or less, depending on freshness. In addition, they are full of calcium, potassium, sodium and phosphorus.

My favorite way to cook an artichoke is to steam it, either in a pressure cooker or just in my vegetable steamer. Test for doneness by piercing with the tip of a knife at the base of the stalk near the heart.

This recipe is from **Bon Appetit,** one of our favorite magazines on food and wine.

½ Cup plus 2 tablespoons (1¼ cubes) unsalted butter
½ Cup carrots, chopped
½ Cup celery, chopped
½ Cup onion, chopped
½ Cup mushrooms, chopped
¼ Cup all purpose flour
1 Cup chicken stock
2 8½ ounce cans quartered artichoke hearts, juice reserved
1 Bay leaf
¾ Teaspoon salt
½ Teaspoon black pepper, freshly ground
¼ Teaspoon ground red pepper
¼ Teaspoon dried thyme or ¾ teaspoon fresh
¼ Teaspoon dried oregano or ¾ teaspoon fresh
¼ Teaspoon ground sage
Pinch of Hungarian sweet paprika
1 Cup whipping cream

Melt 2 tablespoons butter in a large, heavy skillet over medium heat. Add carrots, celery, onion and mushrooms. Saute until vegetables are soft and onion is translucent, about 15 minutes. Set aside. Melt remaining butter in a large stockpot over low heat. Add flour and cook, stirring constantly, five minutes. Stir in vegetables. Add stock in slow steady stream, stirring constantly. Add artichoke hearts with juice, bay leaf, salt, pepper, ground red pepper, thyme, oregano, sage and the paprika. Stir. Increase heat to medium and simmer approximately 30 minutes, stirring occasionally. Beat cream in small bowl just until frothy. Blend into soup. Heat through, do not boil. Discard bay leaf. Adjust seasonings. Serve immediately. Serves: 4.

Crab Chowder

I don't know of any shellfish that doesn't make a wonderful soup: a chowder, a bisque or a gumbo.

Chowder comes from the French word "Chaudiere," which is a large cauldron in which chefs cook their soups and stews, particularly those made with seafood.

Bisque is the culinary name of a puree, or a thick soup. The word is primarily restricted to shellfish soups. Properly made, the shellfish is cooked in a white wine broth; the shells are then removed, crushed and the liquid is strained into the soup. This gives the crab, lobster or shrimp bisque its pinkish color.

Gumbo is the name of the rich creole soup which traditionally contains okra and "file" powder.

This is the recipe I featured when I was a guest chef at the Annual Crab Festival, a fundraiser for the March of Dimes, at Pier 39 in San Francisco. It is quick and easy to prepare and should be served immediately. It is a very rich chowder and only a cup should be served if you are following it with a full dinner.

1 Pound potatoes, peeled
3 Tablespoons butter
3 Ribs celery, chopped
1 Red bell pepper, chopped
1 Green bell pepper, chopped
1 Onion, minced
3 Cups clam broth
2 Cups heavy cream
1 Pound fresh crabmeat, cooked
Salt and pepper, to taste
Cayenne pepper, to taste
Parsley, freshly chopped

Cut potatoes into small cubes. Drop in boiling water until almost done. Remove from water. Melt butter in a saucepan. Add celery, peppers and onion. Saute until vegetables are soft and translucent (10-12 minutes). Add clam broth and cream. Barely bring to a boil and reduce heat. Simmer 5 minutes to blend flavors. Add potatoes, crabmeat and seasonings. Heat an additional five minutes and serve.

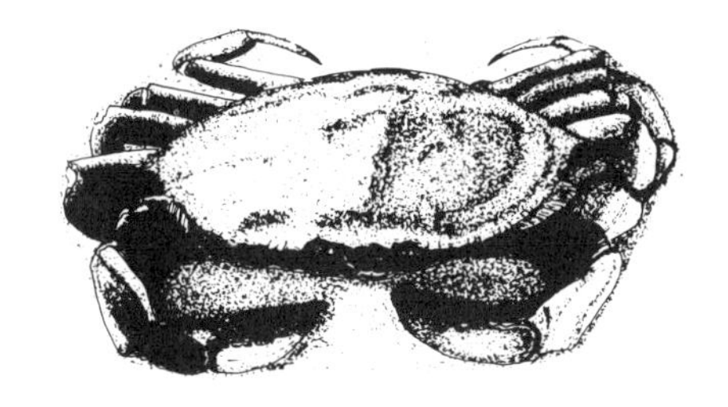

Curried Carrot Soup with Chives

This is a recipe I prepared in January, 1986, for diet month. It is a light soup (only 66 calories), very bright in color and is a wonderful blending of curry and carrots.

It is a recipe from the book "Spa Food" by Edward Safdie. He is the creator of the spa at the Sonoma Mission Inn, just north of San Francisco in the heart of the wine country. The Inn was built in 1926 and the decor reflects a blend of European grand hotel style and country comfort.

The philosophy of healthful eating is simple and based on common sense. Use only the freshest ingredients; emphasize low calorie, low fat foods, whole grains, fresh fruits and vegetables. Practice portion control and use a broad range of foods to make dishes more interesting.

Combined with a regular exercise program, dieting is not that difficult. Reseachers have found that a 24 minute walk after a meal will considerably reduce the impact of the calories consumed, since the combination of eating and exercise speeds up the metabolism.

1 Tablespoon unsalted butter
½ Onion, coarsely chopped
4 Carrots, peeled and coarsely chopped
1 Celery stalk, coarsely chopped
½ Garlic clove, minced
3 Tablespoons curry powder
6 Cups chicken stock
Freshly ground white pepper, to taste
2 Tablespoons chopped chives

In a 3 quart pot, melt the butter. Add the chopped vegetables and garlic. Saute for 4 minutes over medium heat, stirring often. Add the curry powder and cook for additional 3 minutes, stirring constantly. Do not allow the curry to burn. Add the chicken stock. Turn the heat to high and bring to a boil. Lower the heat and simmer, uncovered, for 30 minutes. Puree the soup in several batches in a blender or food processor. Return to the pot. Season to taste. The soup can be made ahead to this point. To serve, reheat the soup, pour into warmed soup bowls and sprinkle with chives. Serves: 4.

Thai Sour Shrimp Soup

Joyce Jue was my guest on the "People Are Talking" show in June, 1983, and prepared Minced Cornish Game Hens with Lettuce Cups (Volume I, P. 156). She returned in May, 1985, to give us another one of her specialties, this hot and spicy shrimp soup from Thailand.

It is very easy to prepare. The most difficult part of this recipe is locating some of the ingredients. Lemon grass stalks are thin, brown reeds about 18" long and have a very strong lemon aroma. They can be found primarily in San Francisco and Oakland Chinatown produce markets. The serrano chilies (very hot) and cilantro can be purchased at any major supermarket. I have found the fish sauce (nam-pla) and dried minced shrimp with chili (sun-dried shrimp chili powder) and coconut milk in the oriental grocery stores.

Joyce still teaches cooking classes in the Bay Area and also offers tours to the Far East on a regular basis. See the Appendix for more information.

2 Tablespoons vegetable oil
½ Pound medium size prawns (keep the shells)
2 Stalks lemon grass, cut into 1" pieces
Zest of a lime
2 Green serrano chilies, cut into slivers
6 Cups chicken stock
1 Teaspoon salt
1 Tablespoon fish sauce
1 Tablespoon lime juice
1 Teaspoon minced dried shrimp with chili
1 Red serrano chili, slivered
1 Tablespoon cilantro leaves, coarsely chopped
2 Scallions, minced
½ Cup coconut milk (optional)

Soup stock: shell and devein the prawns, keeping the shells. In a saucepan, heat the oil. Add the shells and saute for a few seconds until they turn a bright orange. Add the lemon grass, slivered chilies and the zest of a lime. Toss for a few seconds. Add the chicken stock and simmer for 20 minutes. Strain and discard the shells, lemon grass and chilies. Return the stock to a boil. (All of this may be done in advance).

Soup: Bring the stock to a boil. Add the deveined prawns. Simmer for 2-3 minutes or until they are bright orange. Reduce the heat to a simmer and add the salt, fish sauce, lime juice and minced dried shrimp. Remove from heat and stir to combine. Add the slivered red chili. Garnish with cilantro and scallions. Serve hot. Option: warm the coconut milk and add before the cilantro and scallions.

Irish Stew

Many a refined gourmet would wrinkle his nose in disdain at the thought of eating such a lowly dish as lamb stew. And one would imagine that a great master chef would turn up his nose at such an uninspiring dish. Yet, I have known several, who, in the privacy of their own kitchens, prepare and enjoy Irish stew with great enthusiasm!

True Irish stew had mutton as its foundation, but mutton in America is far less tasty than one finds in Great Britain, which is why we use lamb. The simple goodness of lamb with potatoes, onions and carrots make this a taste-tantalizing dish.

This stew is best if prepared a day in advance and refrigerated overnight. Skim off any fat that accumulates on the top before reheating to serve. If your stew is thin and you wish to thicken it, mix together equal parts of soft butter and flour (3 tablespoons each) into a roux. Bring the stew to a boil and mix the roux into the stew, a tablespoon at a time, stirring constantly. Wait until each bit is dissolved before adding more.

2 Pound potatoes, peeled and cubed
4 Large onions, peeled and sliced
3 Pounds lean lamb, cubed
Salt and pepper to taste
½ Teaspoon thyme
2 Bay leaves
6 Carrots, washed and sliced
Fresh parsley, chopped

Place one half of the potatos on the bottom of a 5 quart casserole or dutch oven. Add one half of the sliced onion, then all of the lamb. Season with salt, pepper, thyme and bay leaves. Layer with the remaining onions and then the potatoes. Add just enough water to cover the bottom layer of potatoes, about 2 cups. Stock or broth may be substituted.

Cook stew in a preheated 325° oven for 2 hours. Check from time to time and add hot water if liquid seems to be cooking away. Carrots should be added during the last one half hour to steam on top. Garnish with freshly chopped parsley.

This stew is best if prepared a day in advance and refrigerated overnight. Skim off any fat that accumulates off top before reheating to serve.

Serves: 4 to 6.

Gazpacho

Albert Wilson, "The Gardening Expert," was my guest chef and we prepared this delicious cold vegetable soup. Albert has been appearing on the "People Are Talking" show with Ann and Ross since 1979. His weekly gardening segments demonstrate his knowledge and enthusiasm and cover everything from petunias to plant pests. In addition, Albert offers help to members of the live studio audience who bring sick plants to him for diagnosis.

He is no newcomer to the media. Soon after World War II, he hosted the radio show, "How Does Your Garden Grow" and later moved to television for "Dig It With Albert." Albert's popular book, HOW DOES YOUR GARDEN GROW, is a good resource for any gardener, and is presently in its 11th printing. He suggests, with a chuckle, "It's very risky to garden without my book."

When Albert is not delighting the "People Are Talking" audiences, he conducts weekly gardening classes for senior citizens in the Bay Area. He holds a degree in botany from Stanford University and has focused on sharing his knowledge with others for over 40 years.

1 Large cucumber, pared and halved
2 Large tomatoes, peeled
1 Medium onion, peeled and halved
1 Medium green bell pepper, quartered and seeded
1 Small avocado, sliced
1 Quart tomato juice
1/4 Cup oil (olive or salad)
1/3 Cup red wine vinegar
1/8 Teaspoon tabasco
1½ Teaspoons salt
1/2 Cup toasted croutons
1 Garlic clove, split
1/4 Cup chives, chopped
1 Tablespoon cilantro, chopped

In blender or food processor, combine 1 tomato, ½ the cucumber, ½ the onion, ½ green pepper and 1 cup tomato juice. Cover and blend to puree the vegetables. In a large bowl, mix the pureed vegetables with remaining tomato juice, oil, vinegar, tabasco, salt and pepper. Refrigerate mixture, covered, until it is well chilled, about 2 hours. (Also place 6 serving bowls in refrigerator). Chop remaining tomato, cucumber, onion and green pepper; thinly slice avocado. Place this mixture in chilled bowls. To serve: crush garlic and add to chilled soup. Ladle soup into bowl. Sprinkle with chives, cilantro and croutons.

Vegetable Soup

This is a quick vegetable soup that I prepared during January, my traditional diet month. It contains no salt, as garlic is my salt substitute and it is fairly low in calories. When I prepare the chicken stock*, I do not add salt. If you use a canned broth, be cautious as it is usually pretty salty; I often dilute it by one-half with water.

To keep the soup purely vegetarian, I substitute water for the chicken stock. Any variety of fresh garden vegetables may be used, depending on your personal taste, i.e. chopped spinach or Swiss chard would be a nice addition. Adding rice, barley or pasta shells will increase the calories a little, but would also be a good source of carbohydrates. I add the rice and barley directly to the soup. The pasta, however, should be cooked separately in a large amount of water at a full, rolling boil, drained and added to the soup.

*For homemade chicken stock, see Volume I, p. 26.

¼ Cup vegetable oil
2 Yellow onions, chopped
1 Small stalk celery, chopped
2 Bell peppers, chopped
1 Bunch green onions, chopped
4 Garlic cloves, minced
6-8 Carrots, chopped
½ Cup parsley, freshly chopped
1 Tablespoon Italian seasoning
Freshly ground pepper
4 Potatoes, peeled and cubed
4 Zucchini, cubed
6 Tomatoes, peeled and chopped
8-10 Cups chicken stock

In a large stock pot, heat the oil on high. Add the yellow onions, celery, peppers, green onions, garlic and carrots. Saute 6-8 minutes until soft. Add the parsley, Italian seasoning and pepper. Mix well. Add the potatoes, zucchini, (small yellow crooked squash may also be used) and tomatoes. Cook 2 minutes, stirring until the squash is just heated through. Add the chicken stock. Simmer 1 hour or until the vegetables are tender. Thicken soup by placing 2 or more cups of the vegetables in a food processor or blender and puree. Pour puree back into the soup. Serve hot.

SALADS & SALAD DRESSINGS

Cobb Salad

We serve this famous Hollywood salad during the warm months as a main course. This beautifully arranged salad has a delicious blend of flavors and textures. Present it at the table, then toss and serve at once. A bottle of white wine and a loaf of San Francisco sourdough would round out the meal nicely.

1 Head iceberg lettuce, shredded
Vinaigrette dressing
1 Large tomato, peeled, seeded and chopped
1½ Cups cooked chicken breast, diced
1 Large avocado, peeled, pitted, diced and tossed with 1 tablespoon lemon juice
¾ Pound sliced bacon, crisply cooked, drained and crumbled
2 Hard boiled eggs, chopped
3 Ounces blue cheese, finely crumbled

Place lettuce in a large, wide salad bowl. Pour viniagrette over lettuce and toss well. Spread lettuce evenly in bowl. Arrange tomatoes, chicken, avocado, bacon and eggs in separate wedge-shaped sections on top of the "dressed" lettuce. Place the crumbled cheese in the center. Serve at once.

Vinaigrette Dressing

I wrote in my first cookbook that I always endorse people to make their own salad dressings (p. 53). You select your favorite ingredients, the flavor is better and fresher plus there is quite a substantial dollar savings.

This vinaigrette dressing is similar to the one in Volume I, however, I have added garlic and some dried oregano. If you can find some balsamic vinegar, try it. You will be amazed at the different taste it adds. Remember, proportions of oil and vinegar may be adjusted according to your personal taste; keep in mind that the strength of vinegars varies from one brand to another.

½ Cup plus 2 tablespoons olive oil
⅓ Cup balsamic vinegar
1 Garlic clove, minced
½ Teaspoon dry mustard
¼ Teaspoon dried oregano
Salt and freshly ground pepper, to taste

Combine olive oil with all other ingredients. Whisk well. Set aside and chill. Remove from refrigerator ½ hour before using. Taste for seasonings.

Curried Tuna Salad

Mary's mother's name is Mildred and she lives in Riverside, California. My mother's name is also Mildred and she lives in San Francisco, California. When we are talking about them, we refer to Mary's mom as "Riverside Millie" and my mom as "SFO Millie."

This recipe for curried tuna salad is one of "Riverside Millie's" favorites. She likes it for many reasons... it is high in protein, is economical and tastes absolutely delicious. It also has wonderful textures; the crunch of the celery and almonds contrasts with the crisp, juicy grapes and the tang of the curry. "Riverside" also likes it because it is so versatile. If she doesn't have tuna, she uses some cold chicken breast or turkey and if grapes aren't in season, she'll use raisins.

This is the perfect salad to serve your family on a hot summer day. Either iced tea or white wine would be a good accompaniment.

P.S. Both "Mildred's" were born in Iowa!

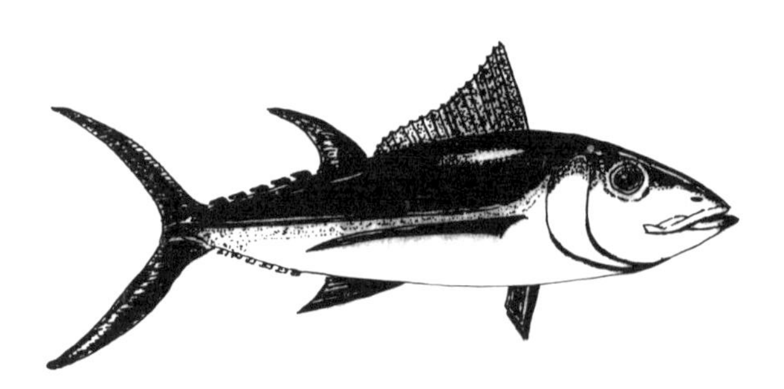

½ Cup small shell macaroni (uncooked)
1 Large apple
1 Tablespoon lemon juice
1 Cup celery, diced
1 Cup seedless grapes, green and red, sliced
2 Green onions, sliced
1 7 ounce can tuna, drained
2 Egg yolks
1 Teaspoon dijon mustard
1 Teaspoon curry powder
¼ Teaspoon ginger
1 Garlic clove
Dash of cayenne pepper
1 Tablespoon lime juice
½ Cup oil, olive or vegetable
½ Cup slivered almonds

Cook, drain and chill macaroni. Peel and dice apple. Mix with the lemon juice in a medium size bowl. Add celery, grapes, onions, macaroni and tuna. Before adding tuna, crumble it into bite-size pieces. In a separate bowl or food processor, blend egg yolks, mustard, curry powder, ginger, garlic, cayenne pepper and lime juice. While stirring continuously, slowly add the oil. Blend well. Mix with the salad. Add ¼ cup almonds. Chill up to two hours before serving. Top with remaining almonds.

C.K.'s Dressing

One day while driving into the city, I was listening to Al Hart and Harvey Steinman of the "KCBS Kitchen," a daily radio talk show about food and wine. On the show, Harvey always offers one of his favorite recipes. As I was crossing the Bay Bridge, he talked about this salad dressing. I frantically tried to write it down and drive at the same time, only to find out that it would appear in the food section of next Wednesday's San Francisco Chronicle. I was much relieved! I clipped it out and tried it at the firehouse. This creamy, garlic, pepper dressing was a big hit with the guys.

2½ Cups mayonnaise
1 Cup sour cream
1 Tablespoon fresh dill, chopped (or 1½ teaspoons dried)
3 Tablespoons Parmesan cheese, freshly grated
2½ Teaspoons pepper, freshly ground
1 Clove garlic
Juice of ½ lemon
1 Tablespoon Worcestershire sauce
2 Teaspoons onion, freshly grated
¾ Tablespoons cider vinegar

Blend all ingredients well. Taste for salt. Yield: 4 cups.

Anchovie Dressing

I mentioned on the show one Tuesday that I like anchovies. The following week in the mail I received this terrific recipe from a viewer.

1 Celery stick, chopped
½ Medium onion, chopped
3-4 Garlic cloves, skinned
1 2 ounce can flat anchovies, drained
1 Teaspoon pepper
½ Teaspoon sugar
2 Tablespoons Dijon mustard
1 Tablespoon lemon juice
3 Eggs
1½-2 Cups salad oil

Puree celery, onion, garlic, anchovies, pepper, sugar, dijon mustard and lemon juice in food processor. Add eggs, one at a time and puree after each addition. Pour salad oil, by droplets at first, and continue with a slow stream until you have the right consistency.

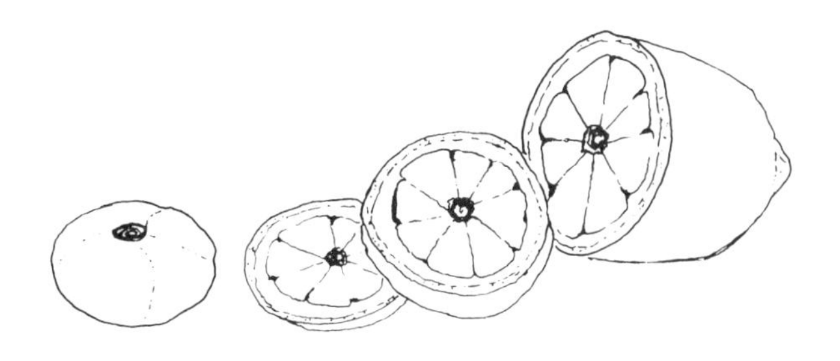

My Aunt's Coleslaw

Jeremiah Tower was my guest chef in the fall of 1986 (see photo page xii). This remarkable young chef is instrumental in transforming the "Chez Pannise" from a Berkeley Cafe to one of the Bay Area's outstanding restaurants. He repeated this accomplishment at the "Balboa Cafe," "Santa Fe Bar and Grill" and "Stars." Jeremiah, a Harvard graduate, was born in the United States and was educated in England and the United States.

In his cookbook, "New American Classics," throughout the first chapter, he tells of his personal favorites; his Aunt's Coleslaw tops the list! He quotes, "The whole key to the success of this salad is to cut the cabbage and tomatoes in large pieces and soak the cabbage in ice water in the refrigerator for 4 hours. The 'dressed' slaw has to sit in the refrigerator for a couple of hours to achieve the perfect blend of flavors and textures".

We prepared this coleslaw and mayonnaise on the show and now it is one my personal favorites!

1 Head white cabbage
4 Large ripe tomatoes
½ Cup mayonnaise
½ Cup sour cream
1 Tablespoon fresh ginger, finely chopped
1 Teaspoon powdered ginger
1½ Teaspoons dry mustard
Salt and freshly ground pepper, to taste

Discard any of the outer leaves of the cabbage that are wilted or discolored. Cut the cabbage in half from top to bottom and cut out the core. Put each half, cut side down, on the cutting board and cut into ½ inch slices. Put the cabbage in a large bowl. Cover with cold water and ice cubes and refrigerate for 4 hours. Peel and seed the tomatoes; cut each tomato half into 6 pieces. Mix the mayonnaise, sour cream, fresh and powdered gingers, and mustard together in a bowl. Drain the cabbage VERY WELL and mix thoroughly with the dressing. Season with salt and pepper. Add the tomatoes and toss lightly. Refrigerate, covered for 2 hours. Serve very cold.

Mayonnaise

3 Large egg yolks
½ Teaspoon salt
4 Tablespoons fresh lemon juice
1-1 ½ Cups olive oil

Put the yolks, salt and half the lemon juice in a bowl and whisk until smooth. Whisk in the oil very slowly at first, increasing the flow at the end. If the mayonnaise gets too thick to beat, add droplets of water and continue adding oil. (The amount of oil will depend on the consistency of mayonnaise desired.) Whisk in the remaining lemon juice and taste for salt.

Pineapple Salads

Pineapples are available the year around and are most abundant from March through June. Living in California we are blessed with frequent shipments from Hawaii and Mexico. All pineapples are picked ripe and will not get any sweeter after harvesting. Look for yellow to golden orange coloring when selecting a pineapple and avoid any with bruises, soft spots or brownish leaves. Since the pineapple will not improve with age, once you buy one, the sooner you eat it the better.

Here are two delicious salads using fresh pineapple that I know you will enjoy!

Hawaiian Pineapple Trade Wind Salad

1 Fresh pineapple
1 Cup cooked chicken breast, shredded
½ Cup green onions, chopped
¼ Cup cashews
½ Cup sour cream
2 Tablespoons vegetable oil
1 Tablespoon white wine vinegar
2 Teaspoons soy sauce
Shredded lettuce

Cut pineapple in half lengthwise through crown leaving shells intact. Refrigerate one half for later use. Remove fruit from remaining half. Remove core and dice fruit. Combine pineapple, chicken, onion and cashews. Spoon back into shell. Combine sour cream, oil, vinegar and soy sauce. Serve over salad. Serve with shredded lettuce.

Pineapple Calypso Salad

½ Large fresh pineapple
½ Cup mushrooms, freshly sliced
½ Cup red onion, thinly sliced
1 Large banana
1 Large tomato
1 Head lettuce (romaine or curly green)
Lime dressing

Remove pineapple from shell. Core and cut fruit into generous wedges. Place in a bowl. Trim and slice mushrooms. Thinly slice onion and add to pineapple. Drizzle 3 tablespoons lime dressing over mixture. Cover and chill. When ready to serve, peel and slice the banana and cut tomato into small wedges. Combine with marinated mixture. Break lettuce into bite-size pieces. Place in a large salad bowl. Spoon pineapple mixture over top. Serve with remaining lime dressing. Serves: 4.

Lime Dressing

3 Tablespoons sugar
½ Teaspoon salt
¼ Teaspoon paprika
3 Tablespoons lime juice, freshly squeezed
1 Tablespoon pineapple juice (from fresh pineapple)
1 Tablespoon light rum (or ½ teaspoon rum extract)
½ Cup vegetable oil
¼ Teaspoon lime rind, freshly grated

Put sugar, salt, paprika, lime juice, pineapple juice and rum into a small bowl or jar. Stir to dissolve the sugar. Add oil and zest of the lime. Whisk or shake well. Yield: Approx. ¾ cup.

Prawn Salad

Shrimp are called prawns in some places and prawns are called shrimp in others; both commonly are known as shrimp in the United States.

Fresh shrimp, also called "green" shrimp, sometimes are marketed with their heads on, especially when sold close to where they are taken. Many gourmet restaurants as far north as New York, Chicago and San Francisco now seek these out for the guarantee of freshness and added flavor they provide in many dishes.

For this recipe, I used the medium shrimp, about 20 to 24 per pound and they may be either fresh or frozen. If you use the frozen, be sure they are well thawed before you cook them.

I featured this recipe in February, 1985 as the first course for the Presidential dinner (see index). This is such a delicious salad, I also like to serve it as an entree with some San Francisco sourdough french bread, a glass of chilled white wine and some rich, chocolate brownies for dessert.

1 Cucumber
Oil
Vinegar
½ Pound prawns
½ Cup mayonnaise
1 Garlic clove, minced
¼ Cup green onions, finely chopped
Cayenne pepper, to taste
Parsley sprigs

Wash cucumber. "Score" lengthwise with a fork. Thinly slice and marinate in a bowl with oil and vinegar (2 parts oil to 1 part vinegar). Season with salt and pepper, to taste. Chill several hours.

Peel and devein prawns. Plunge into salted boiling water for 2½-3 minutes. Drain and chill. Coarsely chop prawns by hand or with a food processor. Add mayonnaise, garlic, onions and cayenne pepper. Blend well. (If mixture seems too dry for your taste, add a bit more mayonnaise.) Chill.

When ready to serve, arrange cucumber slices overlapping each other on a chilled salad plate. Spoon the prawn mixture into the center. Garnish with a sprig of parsley. Serve at once.

Spaghetti di Zucchini

The zucchini is a member of the summer squash family, along with the crookneck, scallopini and the pattypan. They are eaten when they are immature; the skin is fine and thin and the seeds are barely developed. Summer squashes should be cooked quickly. Mixing squashes in a saute pan with a bit of butter, fresh tomato, garlic and basil make a perfect accompaniment to almost any entree.

This recipe is quick and easy to prepare and the result is a marvelous blending of flavors. It is a wonderful, light first course or would make an ideal luncheon entree.

Jim's Featured Pick:

SPEIDINI'S
101 Ygnacio Valley Road
Walnut Creek, CA
(415) 939-2100

2 Large zucchini
½ Cup prosciutto, cut into small strips
1 Lemon
¼ Cup extra virgin olive oil
White pepper, to taste
¼ Cup Parmesan cheese, freshly shredded

Slice zucchini lenthwise, 1/8'' thick. Cut into very thin spaghetti-like strips. Zucchini should equal approximately 2 cups. The ratio should be 4 parts zucchini to 1 part prosciutto. Mix together in a bowl. Squeeze the juice of the lemon on the mixture. Add olive oil and white pepper. Toss until the ingredients are well coated with dressing. To serve: divide evenly on four chilled salad plates. Top with shredded Parmesan cheese. This recipe should be made and served at the last minute. If it is made in advance, the zucchini will become soggy.

Spinach Salad

My daughter, Jennifer, loves spinach salad and insists that the very best she's ever had is at "Catrina's" restaurant on West Winton in Hayward, California. Otto Catrina prepares this sumptuous salad in a chafing dish at your table with flair and enthusiasm. This great salad is easily recreated at home.

2 Bunches spinach
4 Slices lean bacon
1 Tablespoon worcestershire sauce
1 Tablespoon Dijon style mustard
¼ Cup red wine vinegar
¼ Cup sugar
Freshly ground pepper

Clean, wash and dry the spinach. Chill well. Trim the bacon of excess fat. Saute the bacon over medium heat until soft, not crisp. Add worcestershire sauce, mustard, vinegar and sugar. Stir and heat through. Pour over spinach and toss well. Serve with freshly cracked pepper.

String Bean and Mushroom Salad

I created this recipe for a "Diet Month" feature in January, 1987. The variety of colors on the plate make it very eye appealing plus it has only 120 calories per serving. I like to serve it as a first course when beans are abundant from the garden.

1 Pound string beans, trimmed
½ Pound fresh mushrooms
1 Tablespoon Dijon style mustard
2 Tablespoons red wine vinegar
1 Garlic clove, chopped
½ Teaspoon salt
Freshly ground pepper
4 Tablespoons olive oil
¼ Cup parsley, freshly chopped
¼ Cup green onions, chopped

Bring one quart water to a boil. Drop the trimmed beans into it. Leave for 5-7 minutes, uncovered. Drain. Plunge into ice water for 3-4 minutes. Drain and set aside. Wash and dry the mushrooms and thinly slice. Put the mustard, wine vinegar, garlic, salt and pepper into a small mixing bowl. Blend well. Slowly add the olive oil to the mixture, whisking continuously. Put the string beans, mushrooms, parsley and green onions in a salad bowl. Pour the dressing over the vegetables. Toss gently. Serves: 6.

SAUCES

Apricot Bar-B-Que Sauce
Onion Cream Sauce
Beef or Chicken Marinade
Cucumber Sauce
Tomato Pepper Mayonnaise
Little Joe's Tomato Sauce
Slav Sauce
Snail Butter

Apricot Bar-B-Que Sauce

When the bar-b-que season begins in June, apricots are at the peak of their crop. This is the perfect sauce to serve at your first summer party. It is unusual and very delicious!

I like to serve it on chicken, turkey or even pork chops. So often bar-b-qued meats are burnt on the outside and not done on the inside. I always pre-cook my poultry in the oven for about 30 minutes at 350°. Then I place it on the bar-b-que to finish cooking, continuously basting with this sauce.

2 Cups fresh apricots (10), pitted
⅔ Cup apple cider vinegar
⅔ Cup catsup
4 Tablespoons soy sauce
¾ Cup brown sugar
2 Garlic cloves, minced
2 Teaspoons ginger
1 Onion, finely chopped
Freshly ground pepper, to taste

Combine all ingredients in food processor. Puree. Pour into a medium sauce pan. Heat through, over low heat, a minimum of 30 minutes.

Onion Cream Sauce

The first time I prepared Chicken Cordon Bleu I felt that it was too dry. Maybe I overcooked it or let it sit too long before serving... who knows? Anyway, the next time I decided to accompany it with a sauce and created this onion cream sauce. Primarily, I serve it with the Cordon Bleu, but it would also be excellent with any broiled or roasted chicken dish.

1 Large onion, finely chopped
2 Tablespoons butter
¼ Cup white wine
½ Cup chicken broth
½ Cup heavy cream
1 Tablespoon Dijon style mustard
1 Tablespoon parsley, freshly chopped

In a saucepan, saute onion in butter until soft, over medium high heat. Add white wine. Cook until wine is almost evaporated. Add chicken broth and simmer for about 3-4 minutes. Whisk in the heavy cream, mustard and fresh parsley. Heat through. Serve immediately.

Beef or Chicken Marinade

This recipe is from the "Sorabol", a Korean Restaurant in Oakland, California. One of the most popular dishes on their menu is "Bul-Gokee." It is thinly sliced beef or chicken which has been marinating in this sauce for about 15 minutes.

Young-Ran Hong, the hostess and owner, oversees the waitresses who are adorned in authentic Korean style dress, as they cook the entree at the table on a small hibachi style cooker that is piping hot. The chicken and beef are both cooked rapidly.

All the dinners come accompanied with steamed rice and several condiments, some of which are spicy hot with a strong influence of garlic.

Jim's Featured Pick:

SORABOL
372 Grand Avenue
Oakland, CA 94610
(415) 839-2288

1 Cup light soy sauce
2 Teaspoons sesame oil
1 Teaspoon garlic, chopped
1 Teaspoon toasted sesame seeds
2 Teaspoons green onion, chopped
1 Teaspoon rice wine
1 Teaspoon sugar
1 Teaspoon black pepper
½ Cup water

Combine all ingredients. Mix well. Marinate your beef or chicken 15 minutes before cooking. Broil chicken 2 minutes on each side or until done. Broil beef about 1 minute total, depending on the thickness of the slice.

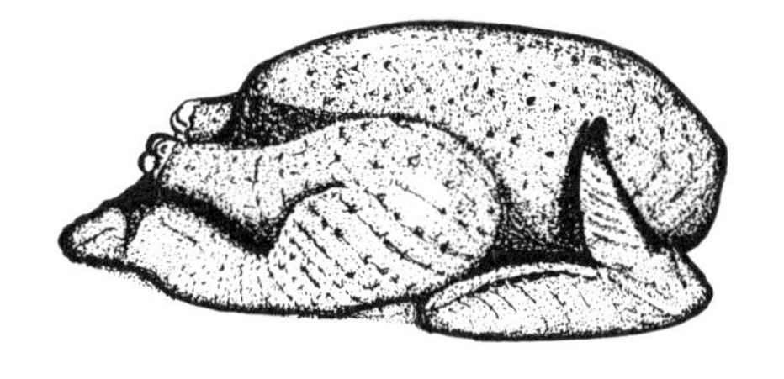

Cucumber Sauce

This is a wonderful, light sauce I prepared on the show to be served with fish filets (page 146). It is crisp, refreshing, low in calories and the tang from the yogurt gives the sauce a Middle Eastern flavor.

1 Cucumber
2 Tablespoons onion, finely chopped
Juice of ½ lemon
1 Tablespoon dill, freshly chopped
Dash of tabasco (optional)
½ Cup plain yogurt
½ Cup imitation sour cream
Salt and pepper, to taste

Wash, seed and coarsely chop cucumber. Combine with onion, lemon juice, chopped dill, tabasco, yogurt, sour cream, salt and pepper. Blend well.

Tomato Pepper Mayonnaise

1 Red bell pepper
1 Tomato
Pinch of cayenne pepper
3 Egg yolks
4 Garlic cloves, well crushed
Juice of ½ lemon
2 Tablespoons vinegar
Salt and pepper, to taste
1½ Cups olive oil

Peel, seed and devein the pepper. Peel, seed and chop the tomato. Put the cayenne pepper, egg yolks, garlic, lemon juice and vinegar into a food processor. Blend. Slowly add the olive oil making a thick mayonnaise. Add the red bell pepper and tomato. Blend. Season with salt and pepper.

Little Joe's Tomato Sauce

"Little Joe's," The Italian Restaurant on Broadway in the heart of San Francisco's North Beach area, has a motto on the door, "Rain or Shine, There's Always A Line." Daily, an average of 1,000 people don't mind the wait to sample Little Joe's Italian cooking.

The owner and founder of the restaurant, Franco Montarello, comes from a small town on the coast of Italy near Genoa. This area is best known for their pesto sauces and ravioli. Franco brought with him all the recipes for the robust sauces and pungent marinades that are evident in the restaurant's favorite dishes. Eating at "Little Joe's" is truly a dining experience to be treasured and remembered!

One of the secrets of all of Franco's sauces is "cooking down." This is known in the kitchen as the "reduction method." The idea is to cook down or reduce the liquids: the wine, broth or water.

Franco has written a cookbook (see appendix) which is a collection of the best recipes from "Little Joe's" kitchen, along with some history, cooking hints and information about finding and using the best ingredients.

Jim's Featured Pick:

LITTLE JOE'S
523 Broadway
San Francisco, CA
(415) 982-7639

2 Quarts crushed tomatoes in heavy puree
2 Quarts chicken broth
4 Stalks celery
3 Onions, finely minced
1 Tablespoon dried ground oregano
1 Teaspoon dried rosemary
4 Bay leaves
2 Tablespoons basil, freshly chopped
¼ Cup minced garlic
2 Tablespoons black pepper
1 Tablespoon salt
½ Cup olive oil
¼ Cup cornstarch, dissolved in ½ cup water
Pasta of choice
Parmesan cheese, freshly grated

It is not necessary to saute any of the items in this recipe. Combine crushed tomatoes, chicken broth, celery, onions, oregano, rosemary, bay leaves, basil, garlic, pepper, salt and olive oil. Bring all ingredients to a boil. Reduce heat. Cook for 2½-3 hours. Thicken with one half cup dissolved cornstarch. Serve over pasta of your choice. Top with Parmesan cheese.

This sauce can be bottled and frozen for later use.

Slav Sauce

My guest chef, Sally Socolich, has been a regular on the "People Are Talking" show since 1978. She is better known as the "Bargain Hunter" and enlightens the television audience weekly with her latest discoveries. Her book, "Bargain Hunting in the Bay Area," has sold over 300,000 copies to date and is currently in its 7th printing. Sally also produces a monthly newsletter which updates subscribers on her most recent finds.

Sally suggests the following strategy for saving money on your food budget. When making casseroles and dishes that freeze well, double or triple the recipe so that you'll always have freezer meals on hand when you're too busy or too tired to cook. Her favorite "fast food" recipe, three gallons of Slav sauce, takes a few hours to prepare, but provides 12-25 meals for her family depending on the size of the freezer portions. This recipe may be reduced by half for those with limited freezer space. This sauce may be served over any pasta, although mostaccioli, rigatoni and raviolis are preferred, while fresh potato gnocchi is her family's favorite.

4 Tablespoons butter
4 Large onions
1 Large bunch fresh parsley
10 Garlic cloves
5 Green bell peppers
10- 12 Pounds of chuck roast, cubed
Olive oil
6 28-ounce cans tomato sauce
1½ Tablespoons cinnamon
3 Tablespoons basil
2 Teaspoons cloves
2 Tablespoons oregano
Salt and pepper, to taste

Finely chop (or process in the food processor) onion, parsley, garlic and peppers. Saute in melted butter until limp. Brown meat in batches in olive oil. Don't drain off cooking oil when finished since you'll be losing the flavorful meat juices. Combine meat and sauteed vegetables. Stir in tomato sauce. Blend well. Add seasonings. Cook mixture over low heat 2½ to 3 hours. Cool to room temperature and skim off fat before putting into freezer containers. Figure ¾ cup sauce per serving.

Snail Butter

Snails are taken very seriously in France where they are called "Escargot." In the springtime, the French gather them in the vineyards after a rainfall and store them in cages for about a week to rid them of impurities. Then they grill them over hot coals, season with salt and pepper, pluck them from their shells, and eat them on French bread which has been smeared with garlic butter.

If you buy fresh snails, you have to purge them of any toxic plants and fatten them on aromatic herbs mixed with cornmeal for at least two weeks, while keeping them in a closed box. They should be washed several times in salted-vinegar water and rinsed well before cooking. I recommend to simply buy the canned variety; all you have to do is drain them! There are, however, snail farms in the San Francisco Bay Area, but I have never visited one or tried any of their snails.

If you have butter leftover, it will keep well in the refrigerator for several weeks. My daughter, Jennifer, and her girlfriend, Karen, cringed at the thought of eating "escargot", they do, however, recommend that the garlic butter is perfect for corn on the cob!

1 Cup butter, unsalted, softened
2 Tablespoons parsley, freshly chopped
1 Tablespoon shallots, freshly chopped
4 Garlic cloves, peeled and crushed
1 Teaspoon Pernod
½ Teaspoon salt
White pepper, to taste
½ Slice white bread, trimmed, cubed and crumbed
1 Tablespoon dry white wine

Combine all ingredients except the bread and wine. Blend the bread and wine until the wine is absorbed. It is good to add some liquid like white wine to the bread because it blends easier with the butter during cooking and also cuts the fattiness of the dish. The bread is added to absorb the wine, which could not be incorporated into the butter when cold. Blend the seasoned butter with the bread/wine mixture. Yield: Enough for about 2 dozen snails.

24 Escargot Shells
24 Escargot

To serve: Place ½ teaspoon of snail butter into an escargot shell or oven-proof escargot serving dish. Place one escargot into the shell. Top with 1 teaspoon of snail butter. Bake in a preheated 375° oven for 10-12 minutes. Let cool 5 minutes before serving.

PASTAS

Garlic Shrimp and Oysters on Pasta

Paul Prudhomme was my guest on the "People Are Talking" show in the fall of 1984. No one is more responsible for expanding and preserving the authentic Cajun and Creole cooking of South Louisiana than Paul. In his book, "Paul Prudhomme's Louisiana Kitchen," Paul states that seafood deserves special attention. This recipe that we prepared shows his skill as a great chef!

Paul has created his own seasoning mixes, called "Cajun Magic," which can be found at most major supermarkets. They can be substituted for the seasoning mix in this recipe.

If you don't have time to prepare the seafood stock, use some bottled clam juice or a concentrated fish bouillon cube.

One thing Paul emphasized was the shaking of the pan in a back and forth motion and the addition of stock to the melting butter. This keeps the sauce from separating and having an oily texture. Stirring does not produce the same effect.

Seafood Stock

1 Medium onion, unpeeled and quartered
1 Large garlic clove, unpeeled and quartered
1 Stalk celery
1½ -2 pounds rinsed shrimp heads and/or shells or crawfish heads and/or shells, or crab shells or rinsed fish carcasses (heads and gills removed) or oyster liquor or any combination of these

Always start with cold water, enough to cover the other ingredients. Place ingredients in a stock pot or a large saucepan. Bring to a boil over high heat. Then gently simmer at least 4 hours, preferably 8 hours, replenishing the water as needed to keep about 1 quart of liquid in the pan. The pan may be uncovered or set a lid on it askew. Strain, cool and refrigerate until ready to use. Note: if you are short on time, using a stock simmered 20-30 minutes is far better than using just water in any recipe.

Garlic Shrimp and Oysters on Pasta Continued

Garlic Shrimp and Oysters on Pasta
Continued

1/2 Pound fresh spaghetti or ⅓ pound dry, cooked
1½ Sticks (3/8 pound) unsalted butter
½ Cup green onions, chopped
8 Peeled medium shrimp (about 3 ounces)
1 Tablespoon garlic, minced
3½ Teaspoons seasoning mix
8 Shucked oysters, drained (we use medium-size ones, about five ounces)
¾ Cup warm seafood stock

Melt 6 tablespoons of the butter in a large skillet over high heat. Add the green onions, shrimp, garlic and the seasoning mix. Cook until shrimp turn pink while vigorously shaking the pan in a back-and-forth motion (versus stirring), about 1 minute. Add the oysters, stock and remaining 6 tablespoons butter. Cook until butter melts and oysters curl, about 1 minute, continuing to shake the pan. Add the cooked spaghetti. Toss and cook until heated through, about 1 minute. Remove from heat and serve immediately. Serves: 2.

Seasoning Mix

¾ Teaspoon salt
½ Teaspoon white pepper
½ Teaspoon onion powder
½ Teaspoon ground red pepper (preferably cayenne)
½ Teaspoon sweet paprika
½ Teaspoon dried thyme leaves
¼ Teaspoon black pepper

Combine the seasoning mix ingredients thoroughly in a small bowl and set aside.

Lasagne

Italians will usually eat a small portion of pasta before the main course. Served properly in a small warmed bowl, its purpose is to whet the appetite. In unusual circumstances, larger portions are served when a special pasta is presented as an entree, such as a lasagne.

My wife, Mary, and I each have our own lasagne recipe. When we decided to prepare it for friends, rather than argue as to whose was the best, we combined recipes.

I insist on making fresh pasta as it is much lighter than the packaged pasta. Also, whenever I serve pasta, I use only freshly grated Parmesan cheese; you really can taste the difference.

Lasagne Continued

Lasagne Continued

Pasta Dough

1½ Cups flour
2 Large eggs
Dash of salt

Combine ingredients in a food processor until blended. If it seems dry, add a few drops of olive oil. If it seems moist, add a bit more flour. Wrap the dough in plastic wrap and let rest for 15 minutes. Thinly roll out the pasta. Slice it into strips to fit the bottom of your baking dish. Cook the fresh pasta for about one minute in boiling salted water. Drain and place on a kitchen towel to dry before using.

Meat Sauce

2 Tablespoons olive oil
2 Tablespoons butter
1 Onion, finely chopped
2 Stalks celery, finely chopped
1 Large carrot, finely chopped
1 Pound extra lean ground beef
1 Cup dry white wine
Salt and freshly ground pepper, to taste
2 Cans tomatoes, Italian style

Melt butter with oil in a large saucepan. Add onion, celery and carrot. Saute over medium heat. Add beef. Cook and stir until meat is no longer pink. Season with salt and pepper. Increase heat and stir in wine. Cook until wine has evaporated. Add tomatoes, cover and reduce heat. Simmer 1 to 1½ hours or until sauce reaches a medium thick consistency, stirring occasionally.

White Sauce

2 **Cups ricotta cheese**
1 **Cup Parmesan cheese, freshly grated**
3 **Eggs**
½ **Cup heavy cream**

Combine all ingredients in blender or food processor and set aside.

To assemble: Preheat oven to 450°. Generously butter a 14 inch bake and serve lasagne-type casserole. Cover bottom with a thin layer of meat sauce. Place a single layer of cooked pasta in the prepared casserole. Spread meat sauce on the pasta, then spread a layer of white sauce. Add another layer of pasta and continue with the layers of meat sauce, white sauce and pasta. Do not make more than 6 thin layers. Use the trimmings to plug up any gaps in the layers. Coat the top layer with the white sauce and dot lightly with butter. If desired, you may sprinkle the top with additional Parmesan or grated mozzarella cheese. Bake on the uppermost rack of the oven for 10-15 minutes. If after 10 minutes baking you see that no crust is beginning to form, raise the oven temperature for the next 5 minutes. Allow lasagne to set 8-10 minutes before serving. Serve directly from casserole.

Modesto Lanzone's Pasta

Modesto Lanzone was my guest chef on the "People Are Talking" show in May, 1985. He came to help promote the Gourmet Gala, an annual fundraising event for the local chapter of the March of Dimes. The event is a black-tie dinner dance which features a competition of celebrity chefs who create their favorite recipe. I thought it was appropriate to have Modesto prepare a pasta dish since he is the owner of two very successful Italian restaurants in San Francisco.

He asked me to have a pot with some boiling water for pasta and to stop at the local supermarket and buy some vegetables that were readily available. I bought my favorites... peppers, onions and garlic! He brought some prosciutto and a jar of imported Italian green tomatoes (pomodori verdi). It was "on the air" that we created this pasta dish which is absolutely marvelous!

I have found that the "pomoderi verdi" are not always readily available. Therefore, when you find them at your supermarket or Italian deli, buy a couple of jars. Sun-dried red tomatoes may be used as a substitute, however, use only about ⅔ of a cup.

MODESTO LANZONE'S
Ghiradelli Square
900 North Point
San Francisco, CA
(415) 771-2880

Opera Plaza
601 Van Ness Avenue
San Francisco, CA
(415) 928-0400

⅓ Cup olive oil
2 Garlic cloves, mashed
1 Small yellow onion, chopped
½ Green bell pepper, chopped
½ Red bell pepper, chopped
½ Yellow bell pepper, chopped
½ Cup Prosciutto ham, cubed
1 Cup Italian imported green tomatoes, coarsely chopped
¼ Pound fresh pasta
Parmesan cheese, freshly grated

Heat olive oil in a saute pan. Add garlic and onion. Cook until limp. Add green, red and yellow bell peppers. Saute an additional 5-6 minutes. Add the prosciutto, Parmesan cheese and tomatoes. Heat thoroughly.

Cook pasta in plenty of unsalted boiling water until "Al Dente." Drain.

To serve: Coat pasta with sauce and top with additional Parmesan cheese.

Pasta with Garlic and Apricots

When asked to do a demonstration at the annual Gilroy Garlic Festival, this was the first recipe that came to mind. It's easy to prepare and utilizes two ingredients that are readily available in the central California Valley, garlic and apricots. It sounds like an unusual combination, but the sauteed garlic sweetens in the oil and butter and blends well with the apricots and rosemary. This is a sauce for pasta that does not require Parmesan cheese.

I prefer to serve this as a side dish. A perfect accompaniment would be roasted chicken or grilled pork chops and a bottle of chilled California dry white wine.

2 Tablespoons olive oil
¾ Cup butter, unsalted
20 Garlic cloves, peeled and chopped
1 Cup white wine
2 Tablespoons fresh rosemary
1 Cup dried apricots, chopped
Salt and pepper, to taste
1 Pound pasta
½ Cup parsley, freshly chopped

Heat olive oil and butter in a saute pan. When hot, add garlic and saute over medium heat until soft. Be cautious as to not let the garlic burn or brown. Add wine and simmer, on low heat, uncovered for about five minutes. Add rosemary and apricots. Season with salt and pepper. Simmer for an additional 15-20 minutes.

Cook pasta in plenty of boiling water, until "Al Dente." Drain. Pour into a heated pasta bowl and coat well with sauce. Garnish with freshly chopped parsley. Serve at once.

Pasta Verdi

Many cookbooks credit Marco Polo with bringing spaghetti to Italy from China. But this is just a legend, and is not true. Marco Polo lived from 1254 to 1323 and by the year 1200 the food was well known in Italy and was even mentioned in an historical document!

But if you like legends, you'll get a kick out of this one. One day, hundreds of years ago, a young Chinese maiden was busy preparing her daily batch of bread dough. Becoming engrossed in conversation with an ardent Italian sailor, she forgot her task. Presently dough overflowed from the pan and dripped in strings that quickly dried in the sun. When he observed what had happened, the young Italian, hoping to hide the evidence of his loved one's carelessness, gathered the strings of dried dough and took them back to the ship. The ship's cook boiled them in a broth. He was pleased to find that the dish was appetizing and savory. Upon the ship's return to Italy, word of the delicious new dish spread rapidly, and soon it was popular throughout the land.

This recipe is one of the simplest and yet one of the most impressive pastas, and in my opinion, one of the tastiest!

6 Tablespoons butter, unsalted
2 Tablespoons olive oil
4 Garlic cloves, mashed
¼ Cup Italian parsley, minced
¼ Cup fresh basil, chopped
1 Pound spaghetti
Freshly ground pepper, to taste
¼ Cup Parmesan cheese, freshly grated

Heat butter and oil in a saucepan. Add garlic. Saute until it is soft, being careful not to burn it. Stir in the parsley and basil. Simmer for 3-4 minutes. Cook spaghetti in plenty of boiling water until "Al Dente." Drain. Place in a preheated pasta bowl. Pepper, to taste. Add Parmesan cheese and toss well. Pour hot butter/parsley/basil mixture over pasta and toss again. Serve immediately. Pass extra Parmesan cheese.

Penne Alla Boscaiola

''Penne,'' translated as 'pens' or 'feathers' are short pasta tubes cut diagonally at both ends, like a quill pen. ''Pennine'' (small penne) and ''pennone'' (large penne) are also made ''rigati'' (grooved).

This is a very rich pasta dish and if it is to be served as a first course, I recommend half servings, if I use this as a main course, I precede it with only a tossed green salad. Either a bottle of Italian red or white wine could accompany this dish.

The penne should be cooked separately in a large pot of boiling water. The rule of thumb is seven quarts of water to one pound of pasta. Add 2 tablespoons of salt after the water come to a boil. Add pasta immediately. Test for doneness two or three times during the cooking process, as every pasta is different. The pasta should have no flavor of flour and be biteable, ''Al Dente'' (to the tooth), still firm and chewy.

Jim's Featured Pick:

SANTINO'S
1115 3rd Street
San Rafael, California
(415) 459-4447

2 Tablespoons butter
½ Onion, finely chopped
½ Cup veal, cubed
¼ Cup pancetta, diced
¼ Cup prosciutto, diced
1 Cup mushrooms, sliced
½ Cup dry red wine
4 Italian tomatoes, peeled, seeded and chopped
1 Cup heavy cream
Parmesan cheese, freshly grated
½ Pound of penne, cooked

Melt butter in a saute pan. Add onion and saute until browned. Add veal, pancetta, prosciutto and mushrooms. Saute for ten minutes. Add red wine. Reduce until evaporated. Add tomatoes and cream. Cook an additional 5 minutes on high heat. Serve immediately on prepared pasta. Top with freshly grated Parmesan cheese. Serves: 2 generously.

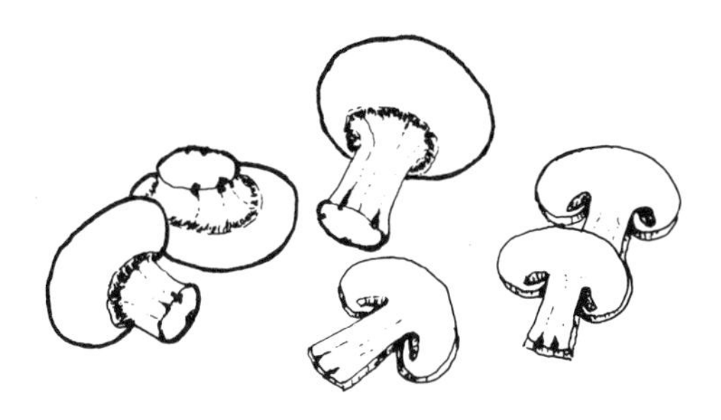

BREADS

Baking Powder Biscuits

When I was growing up my Mom would, at least once a week, prepare baking powder biscuits. She would start about 20 minutes before meal time and magically, as we sat down to dinner. Mom would place hot biscuits on the table! She never seemed to measure any of the ingredients and yet they always came out perfect... about 2 inches high, light, and crusty brown on the top.

The "People Are Talking" show is aired before a live studio audience every day at 10:00 a.m. When I planned to go away on vacation, my producer asked me to tape a cooking segment to be aired the week I was to be out of town. My featured recipe that week was Baking Powder Biscuits. At about 9:00 a.m., Ann and I prepared the dough, cut the biscuits and put them in the oven. We then proceeded to tape the segment, timing it so I could take the hot biscuits out of the oven "on the air." Our timing was perfect, however, the biscuits were hard, dark brown and looked like hockey pucks! It was then that I realized that the baking powder at the T.V. station kitchen had been there for seven years! Moral of the story: check your baking powder. All baking powder has an expiration date on the can and should not be used after that date.

P.S. They never aired that show!

2 Cups flour, sifted
3 Teaspoons baking powder
1 Teaspoon salt
6 Tablespoons shortening
⅔ Cup milk

Preheat oven to 450°. Sift dry ingredients into bowl. Add shortening. Blend with a pastry blender until the mixture is the consistency of meal or bread crumbs. Add milk to make a soft dough. The dough should leave the side of the bowl and not be sticky. Turn dough onto a floured board and knead about 10 times. Roll or press out to ½ inch thickness. Cut with a floured biscuit cutter and place on an ungreased cookie sheet. Bake 10-12 minutes. Yield: 1 dozen large or 18 small biscuits.

Variation: For a sweeter dough (e.g. strawberry shortcake) add 2 Tablespoons of sugar to the flour mixture.

Date Walnut Bread

This is my Aunt Serene's favorite quick bread recipe and has also been a holiday tradition in our family for many years.

I usually start my holiday baking around the first week of December. I make a dozen or so loaves of this bread and put them in the freezer. If you prefer, you may substitute pecans for the walnuts. Either would be great sliced and served warm with a softened cream cheese.

I think it's fun to give and receive gifts of food during the holidays. Mary will wrap the individual loaves in bright red cellophane and tie with a Christmas ribbon... a perfect gift!

1 Cup dates
1 Cup boiling water
1 Teaspoon baking soda
1 Cup sugar
2 Tablespoons butter
1 Egg
1¼ Cup flour
½ Cup walnuts, chopped

Chop dates into small pieces. Place in a small bowl and sprinkle with baking soda. Add boiling water and let stand 15 minutes. In food processor or mixer, cream the sugar and butter. Add the egg. Blend. Fold the flour and chopped nuts into the creamed mixture. Add the dates and baking soda. Stir well. If the mixture looks thin, DO NOT add more flour as this is the way it should look. Grease two 9x5 loaf pans or 4 mini loaf pans. Pour in the batter. Bake in a preheated 350° oven for 30-45 minutes depending on the size of the pans. Test with a toothpick inserted into the center. Let cool before wrapping or freezing.

Dilly Bread

My oldest brother, Joe, is retired from the United States Air Force and lived in northern California near the mouth of the Klamath River. During the late summer and early fall months, when the steelhead salmon migrate upstream, I would always arrange my firehouse schedule or vacation to spend a few days fly fishing with him. After a long day on the river, we would return to his home in the woods to the smell of freshly baked bread. Joe's wife, Hallie, always had two or three loaves cooling on a rack in the kitchen. Soon after our return, we'd have a cup of hot herbal tea and thick slices of warm dilly bread with honey while we told of the big one that got away!

1 Package yeast
¼ Cup warm water
1 Cup cottage cheese
1 Tablespoon butter
2 Tablespoons sugar
1 Tablespoon minced onion
2 Teaspoons dill seed
1 Egg, unbeaten
1¾ to 2 Cups all purpose flour
1 Teaspoon salt
¼ Teaspoon baking soda

Dissolve yeast in warm water. Heat cottage cheese to lukewarm. Combine with yeast mixture. Add the rest of the ingredients. Let rise in warm place 50-60 minutes. Stir down dough. Turn into a well greased 8 inch round casserole. Let rise 30-40 minutes. Bake at 350° for 40-50 minutes. Cover top of bread with foil the last 15 minutes of baking. When done, remove from oven. Brush top of loaf with butter. Sprinkle lightly with salt (optional).

Honey Wheat Bread

Whole wheat flour is different in texture from whole meal flour or whole wheat meal. The latter two are much more coarsely ground and contain rough bits of bran and crushed kernels. Whole wheat kernels contain the bran, the germ, the gluten, everything. Some people like it whole, rather than ground in bread, as it adds texture. Others eat the whole kernels as a cereal. Cracked wheat is merely a coarsely ground whole wheat which is commonly used in cereals but when added to bread, adds a crunchy texture and a nutty flavor.

For yeast to become activated, it must have something to feed on. Give it a little sugar and the yeast cells are encouraged to go to work. Thus, when a sweetener is called for in a bread recipe, it's not simply for flavor. Granulated white sugar is most often used, but molasses, brown sugar and honey may also be used.

1 Cup milk
2 Tablespoons sugar
1 Teaspoon salt
¼ Cup butter
¼ Cup honey
1½ Cup warm water (110-115°)
2 Packages yeast
6 Cups whole wheat flour
2 Tablespoons butter, melted

Heat milk until hot. Add sugar, salt, ¼ cup butter and honey. Stir until butter melts. In a large mixing bowl, add yeast to warm water. Stir until dissolved. Stir in milk mixture. Gradually add flour and mix by hand until the dough forms a ball (more or less flour may be needed). Knead until smooth (about 10-12 minutes) either by hand or machine. Place in a greased bowl. Cover and let rise in a warm place until double (about 1¼ hour). Punch down dough. Turn out onto a floured surface. Divide in half. Shape into two loaves. Place in greased 9x5 bread pans. Brush with melted butter. Cover and let rise again about one hour. Bake 40-50 minutes in a preheated 400° oven. Bread is done, when tapped, it sounds hollow. Remove from pans immediately. Cool on racks.

Monkey Bread

When I prepared this recipe on the show I asked if any of the viewers knew why it was called "Monkey Bread." The most popular answer was that the small clumps of dough are shaped like a monkey's fist. Another viewer referred to the bread as "Bubble Bread" or "Bubble Loaf" because of its bubbly look when it's taken from the oven. Maybe the bread has a silly name because it has a silly shape! Whatever the reason, it is a delicious, sweet bread that is always appreciated when served. I usually serve it warm, with softened butter, for a weekend brunch. Kids especially love it when you let them pull it apart, rather than slice it.

Take special care in the baking to be sure it is thoroughly cooked before it comes out of the oven. Tap the top; it should sound hollow when it's done. If the top browns a little too much, don't worry, because this bread is served inverted.

2 Packages yeast
½ Cup warm water
1 Cup sugar
1 Cup butter
1½ Tablespoons salt
1 Cup milk
3 Eggs plus 2 egg yolks
6 Cups flour
½ Cup brown sugar
½ Cup raisins
1 Tablespoon cinnamon

Dissolve yeast in warm water (100-115°). In a small saucepan, combine sugar, ½ cup butter, milk and salt. Heat and stir until the butter is melted. Remove from heat. Add eggs, extra yolks and yeast mixture. Blend. Combine with flour. Knead dough by hand or in a mixer with a dough hook attachment or in 2 batches in a food processor. Dough should be elastic and smooth. Place in a bowl and set in a warm place to rise until doubled (about 1½ hours). Melt ½ cup of butter with the brown sugar, raisins and cinnamon. Butter an angel food cake pan. When dough has doubled, remove from bowl. Pinch off a piece and roll into a 2" ball. Roll the ball in the butter/brown sugar mixture and place in the cake pan. Continue to arrange in loose layers until dough is used. Let rise again for about 30 minutes or until the dough has almost risen to the top of the pan. Bake in a preheated 375° oven for an hour. Let cool before inverting onto a serving plate. To serve: either slice or let each guest break off individual "balls" of bread.

Popovers

Popovers have become very popular in many restaurants in the Bay Area over the last few years. Most people would never attempt to bake them at home because they seem very difficult. On the contrary... they are very easy to prepare. All you need is a few basic ingredients and a muffin tin. Here's a few helpful tips:

Do not over beat your batter
Yes, your batter will be thin
Preheat your muffin tins and brush with butter
(You can also purchase special popover tins at a cookware store)
Make sure your oven is preheated to 450°
Time them to come out of the oven so they can be placed on the table piping hot

I always serve popovers when I cook a prime rib or standing rib roast instead of making yorkshire pudding. I think they are best with just some soft butter.

1 Cup all purpose flour* (sifted)
1 Tablespoon butter, melted
1 Cup milk
¼ Teaspoon salt
2 Eggs

Put all ingredients in a large bowl or a one quart measuring cup. Mix thoroughly. Pour into preheated, buttered muffin tins or popover pans. Fill only half full. If pans are too full, your popovers will have the consistency of muffins. Bake in a preheated 450° oven for 15 minutes, then reduce the heat to 350° and bake for an additional 20 minutes. Remove from oven and serve immediately. They should be crisp on the outside and moist and tender on the inside.

*For whole wheat popovers, use ⅔ cup whole wheat flour and ⅓ cup all purpose flour.

TRUCK
2
SFFD

MEATS

Beef Stew
Braised Veal Shanks
El Rancho Casserole
Crown Roast of Pork With Stuffing
Grilled Pork Chops
Lamb Shanks
Lamb Chops With Mustard Sauce
Meat Loaf
Mu Shu Pork
Pork Loin Braised In Milk
Pork Tenderloin With Mustard Sauce
Rack of Lamb With Garlic And
  Rosemary
Sauerbraten
Short Ribs In Beer
Veal Picatta
Veal Madeleine

Beef Stew

This is an old-fashioned dish that is especially lovely in the winter and particularly helpful to your pocket book when you buy the meat on sale. I prepare this often at the firehouse where it is always well received.

You may use any portion of the chuck, the largest of the forequarter cuts of beef. These may be labeled as a shoulder, a cross rib or a blade cut, just to name a few. Forequarter cuts are juicy and flavorful and take well to braising, pot-roasting and stewing as they do not get dry or tough with long cooking.

Stewing, a moist-heat method of cooking, is simply cooking meat and or vegetables in liquid in a closed pot or casserole for a relatively long period of time. The result is a delicious blend of a variety of flavors.

3 Cups beef broth
3 Cups red wine
1 Cup port wine
1 Large onion, chopped
3 Stalks celery, chopped
2 Medium carrots, chopped
1 Bay leaf
1 Teaspoon bouquet garni seasoning
4 Thick slices of bacon
3 Tablespoons butter
3-4 Pounds lean beef stew meat
¼ Cup flour
Salt and pepper
3 Garlic cloves, mashed
½ Teaspoon thyme
24 Baby white onions, peeled
1 Pound mushrooms, sliced
¼ Cup tomato puree

In a small stock pot, combine beef broth, red wine, port, onion, carrots, celery, bay leaf and seasonings. Bring to a boil. Reduce to simmer and cook for about 1 hour. Strain and discard vegetables and bay leaf.

Cut bacon into ¼ inch strips. Put into a small saucepan and cover with water. Bring to a boil for 5 minutes (this will remove the salty smokey taste). Drain.

In an oven proof casserole or dutch oven, melt butter. Add bacon. Cook until crisp. Remove with a slotted spoon and place on a paper towel. Brown meat in bacon-butter drippings a few cubes at a time. When all the meat is browned, return it to the dutch oven. Dust with ¼ cup of flour and season with salt and pepper. Stir. Add tomato puree, bacon, garlic and beef wine stock. Cover and cook in oven for 2 hours at 350°. Add onions and mushrooms last ½ hour. Let stew set ½ hour before serving. I think it is best when made a day in advance and reheated. Serve with steamed carrots and boiled new potatoes. Note: Before serving, skim any grease off top.

Braised Veal Shanks

Veal can be sauteed, braised, fried, stewed, roasted or poached. A popular example of a braised dish is Veal Shanks (Osso Buco). Braising can turn the fibrous toughness of the less expensive cuts of veal into a very delicious, tender entree.

The most common accompaniment to Osso Bucco is Risotto (Page 200).

4 Tablespoons butter, unsalted
1½ Cups onions, finely chopped
½ Cup carrots, finely chopped
½ Cup celery, finely chopped
1 Teaspoon garlic, finely chopped
6-7 Pounds Veal Shanks
Salt
Freshly ground pepper
Flour
½ Cup olive oil
1 Cup dry white wine
½ Teaspoon dried basil
¾ Cup beef or chicken stock
½ Teaspoon dried thyme
3 Cups canned whole tomatoes, drained
6 Parsley sprigs
2 Bay leaves

Gremolata

1 Tablespoon grated lemon peel
1 Teaspoon garlic, finely chopped
3 Tablespoons parsley, finely chopped

Choose a heavy, shallow casserole that has a tight cover and is just large enough to hold the pieces of veal in 1 layer. Melt the butter in the casserole over moderate heat. Add the onions, carrots, celery and garlic. Cook, stirring occasionally, for 10-15 minutes, or until the vegetables are lightly colored. Remove from heat. Season the veal with salt and pepper, then roll in flour. Shake off excess. In a heavy skillet, heat 6 tablespoons of olive oil over moderately high heat. Brown veal shanks, adding more oil as needed. Transfer the browned pieces to the casserole on top of the vegetables. Preheat the oven to 350°. Discard almost all of the fat from the skillet, leaving just a film on the bottom. Pour in the wine and boil briskly over high heat until it is reduced to about ½ cup. Scrape in any browned bits clinging to the pan. Stir in the beef or chicken stock, basil, thyme, tomatoes, parsley and bay leaves. Bring to a boil. Pour over the veal. (The liquid should come halfway up the side of the veal. If it does not, add more stock). Bring the casserole to a boil on top of the stove. Cover and bake for approximately 1 ¼ hours. To serve, arrange the veal on a heated platter and spoon the sauce and vegetables around it. Top with gremolata.

El Rancho Casserole

My guest chef, Coreen Cordova, appears regularly on "People Are Talking" as the show's make-up and skin care expert. Coreen is one of the most successful make-up specialists in the Bay Area. She now heads her own corporation and is the owner of a very successful luxurious cosmetic salon in San Francisco.

In her spare time, Coreen devotes her energy to developing make-up techniques for burn patients at St. Francis Hospital Burn Center and also with the Northern California Burn Council.

"Beauty", according to Coreen, "comes from within. You can't paint a smile on with a lipstick or create a sparkle in your eyes with eyeshadow. If you care and feel good about yourself, it shows through in the form of beauty. Make-up is simply a tool for getting your beauty message across."

This recipe has been in Coreen's family for many years. It is a perfect meal for the younger members of the family to help Mom prepare.

1 Pound ground beef
1 Package taco mix
½ Cup onion, chopped
¼ Cup green pepper, chopped
1 10½ ounce can whole kernel corn
1½ Cups Monterey Jack cheese, diced
1½ Cups chili sauce
1 7 ounce can diced green chilies
½ Teaspoon salt
½ Teaspoon cumin powder
¼ Teaspoon chili powder
8 Tortillas
Sour cream

Brown ground beef. Drain. Add taco mix to mixture, adding the liquid per the package directions. In a separate skillet, brown chopped onion and green pepper in a little oil. Saute 2-3 minutes or until the onion is transparent. Add to taco beef mixture. Add corn (undrained), Jack cheese, chili sauce, salt, cumin and chili powder. In a round casserole dish (size of the tortillas) layer the mixture between 8 tortillas evenly, adding diced chilis with each layer. On the top layer, sprinkle generously with additional grated Jack cheese. Bake 30 minutes at 350°. Remove from oven and let stand 10 minutes before serving. Cut in wedges and top with sour cream.

Crown Roast of Pork With Stuffing

I think one of the most magnificent and sumptuous entrees is a crown roast of pork. It is made up of pork ribs, turned and tied to resemble a crown. Each portion is actually a rib chop and the roast can be constructed of any number of chops to serve a moderate size family or a number of guests. It is easy to carve and the center can be heaped with your favorite stuffing, rice or just an apple.

I allow two chops per person, with a few extra for really hearty eaters. Select meat that is firm and lean. Pork may be a bit pink in the center; the key is that the internal temperature must reach a minimum of 140°. Remember, too, that all meats continue to cook, even after they are removed from the oven.

Included with the recipe is my favorite stuffing, a perfect accompaniment to this entree.

1 5 pound center cut pork loin
1 Apple
3 Garlic cloves
Fresh Rosemary sprigs
Salt and pepper, to taste

Have the butcher prepare roast in a crown shape. A pork roast may also be cooked flat without tying into the crown shape. Coarsely chop one apple and place into the center of the roast. Add whole garlic cloves and rosemary. Season with salt and pepper. Roast in a 375° preheated oven for 1 hour 20 minutes. Let rest 15 minutes before serving.

Jim's Stuffing

2 Italian sausages, mild or hot
1 Cup onion, finely chopped
1 Cup celery, finely chopped
¼ Cup fresh parsley, chopped
1 Garlic clove, chopped (optional)
1 Tablespoon olive oil
1 Tablespoon butter
1 Tablespoon Italian seasoning
2 Large apples, coarsely chopped
¼ Cup raisins
2 Cups fresh bread crumbs
½ Cup chicken broth
½ Cup dry white wine
Salt and pepper, to taste

Remove casings from sausage and cook in fry pan over medium heat. Crumble into small pieces while frying. When crisp, remove to a paper towel and drain. In the same pan, add olive oil and butter. Saute onions, parsley, celery and garlic over medium high heat. Cook until vegetables are limp. Set aside and let cool while you peel, core and chop the two apples. In a large bowl, mix the sausage, vegetables and bread crumbs. Stir well. Add the seasonins, apples and raisins. Moisten with the chicken stock and wine. (If you feel the stuffing is too dry, add a little bit of water.) Salt and pepper, to taste. Place in a buttered casserole and bake, lightly covered with foil, in a 375° oven for 1 hour.

Grilled Pork Chops

Mary was born and raised on a farm near Glidden, Iowa. In the summer of 1986, we went back to visit her family and also to celebrate her 25th high school reunion.

This was my first trip to Iowa, so I tried everything from driving the tractors and feeding pigs to riding horses and pulling weeds out of the corn. I have never seen so many acres of corn and soybeans in my life!

Mary's brother John and brother-in-law, Harold, both raise hogs for market. So, needless to say, we ate our share of fresh pork while we were there. They have a cut called the "Iowa chop". It is cut from the center loin and carefully trimmed, weighs 12-16 ounces and is 1¼ to 1½ inches thick, about twice as thick as an ordinary chop and is fresh, not smoked or cured. Iowa chops are by no means exclusive to Iowa, so ask your butcher for a chop which meets these specifications. They're perfect for grilling or stuffing (Volume I, Page 120-121).

When I prepared the chops on the show, I included my recipe for homemade applesauce.

4 **Iowa chops**
½ **Cup butter, unsalted**
2 **Garlic cloves, crushed**
1 **Tablespoon fresh rosemary**
Salt and pepper, to taste

Place butter, garlic and rosemary into a small sauce pan over medium heat. When butter has melted, reduce heat and simmer for 5-7 minutes. Baste chops on each side while grilling.

Applesauce

2 **Pounds Gravenstein apples**
Juice of 1 lemon
½-1 **Cup sugar**
4 **Tablespoons butter, unsalted**
¼ **Teaspoon salt**
1½ **Teaspoons cinnamon**

Peel, core and coarsely chop the apples. Place in a saucepan. Squeeze the juice of the lemon on top. Add ½ cup of water and mix in the remaining ingredients. Cover and cook on low heat 20-30 minutes until apples are soft. Stir occasionally, taking caution that the water does not evaporate. More sugar may be added if desired. Serve hot or cold.

Lamb Shanks

The term, lamb shank, applies to the fore shank of the front leg of the lamb. The shank of the hind leg is left attached and sold as the whole leg of lamb.

When they are cooked over gentle heat, the shanks release enough liquid so that they are braised in their own juices. Maintaining low, even heat is critical to success and make sure you have a tight fitting lid to prevent evaporation. Because of the small amount of liquid, the flavors and seasonings concentrate in deposits left in the pan during the cooking process. These can be easily scraped off the bottom of the pan when you deglaze with the wine.

Lamb shanks are not a fancy cut of meat, but when properly prepared, they are delicious and help keep the budget in good trim. I cook them at the firehouse when ever I can find twelve of them in the butcher's case. Figure on at least one per person and accompany it with a rice dish and some sauteed zucchini with onions.

4 Lamb shanks
4 Tablespoons olive oil
6 Garlic cloves
Salt and pepper, to taste
1 Tablespoon oregano
½ Cup dry white wine

In a large, heavy skillet that has a lid, brown the lamb shanks on all sides in 4 tablespoons olive oil. Add 6 unpeeled garlic cloves, the oregano, salt and pepper. Cover and cook over a very low heat 1½ to 2 hours. When the juices have evaporated and the shanks begin to sizzle in fat, begin to add a spoonful of water from time to time so that a film of liquid always remains in the bottom of the pan. As the meat approaches the desired tenderness, stop moistening with water so that all the liquid will evaporate. When the meat begins to sizzle again in pure fat, remove it to a plate. Pour off the fat and deglaze the pan with the white wine, scraping and stirring with a wooden spoon to dissolve all caramelized adherences. Press the liquid and garlic through a sieve to strain out the garlic skins. Return the liquid to the pan and reduce it to the bubbling stage. Return the meat to the pan; there should be only enough sauce to coat the meat. To serve, top with freshly ground pepper, to taste.

Lamb Chops With Mustard Sauce

When buying lamb, look for lamb that has light, red meat. The one quarter to one half inch of fat covering the outside of the meat should be firm and white, not oily or brittle. You should be able to see some red in the bones; if they are white and bleached, the lamb is old.

I have always enjoyed the taste of lamb and am constantly looking for and trying new ways to prepare it. This recipe is one of my favorites. I like the consistency of the creamy mustard sauce combined with the zest of the cayenne pepper.

When I serve this entree, I accompany it with a tossed green salad with vinaigrette dressing (page 39) and sauteed seasonal vegetables.

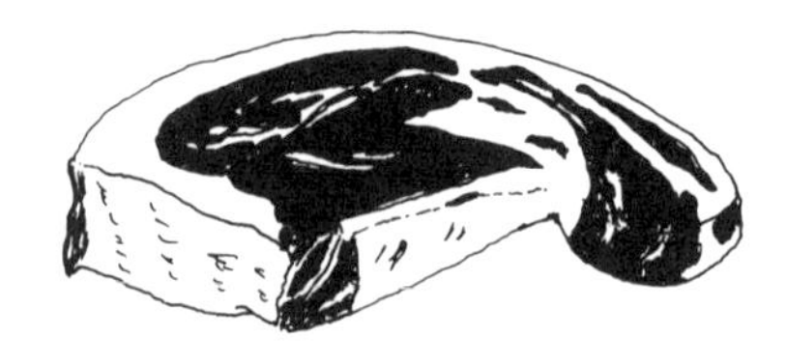

6 Lamb chops, 3 ounces each
2 Tablespoons olive oil
Salt and pepper, to taste
6 Green onions, chopped
¼ Cup white wine
2 Tablespoons Dijon mustard
Cayenne pepper, to taste
½ Cup chicken broth
¼ Cup heavy cream
2 Tablespoons sweet butter

Heat large skillet with olive oil. Season lamb chops with salt and pepper. Saute on each side until done. Remove to a warm platter. Drain oil from skillet. Add half the green onions for five seconds. Deglaze the skillet with wine. Add mustard, cayenne pepper, and chicken broth. Reduce for 20 seconds. Add heavy cream and whisk for additional 10 seconds. Add butter and whisk until incorporated. Taste for seasonings.

Meat Loaf

When I was growing up, I remember having meat loaf about once or twice a month. It was Mom's way of stretching the food dollar. It is made from cheaper cuts of beef, pork and veal ground together. The aroma that came from the kitchen while the meatloaf was cooking was tantalizing and I was drooling when I sat down to the table. If there was ever any left, I always looked forward to meat loaf sandwiches for lunch the next day.

Parslied new potatoes or buttered noodles sprinkled with grated Parmesan cheese go beautifully with this meat loaf. Serve the same dry red wine as was used in preparation of the entree.

Tomato Sauce

½ Cup chili sauce
1 15½ ounce can solid pack tomatoes
¼ Cup red wine garlic vinegar
½ Teaspon chili powder
1 Teaspoon Dijon mustard
2 Teaspoons worcestershire sauce
1 Finely chopped onion
1 Minced garlic clove

Put all ingredients into a saucepan. Simmer for an hour while the meat loaf is baking. Add drippings from roasting pan. Reduce an additional 10 minutes. Pour over sliced meat loaf.

1 Pound ground beef
1 Pound ground pork
1 Pound ground veal
1 Large onion, finely chopped
1 Small green pepper, finely chopped
2 Celery stalks, finely chopped
¼ Cup fresh parsley, finely chopped
½ Pound mushrooms, thinly sliced
1 Cup fresh bread crumbs
½ Cup Madeira wine
3 Eggs, beaten lightly
½ Cup dry red wine
2 Garlic cloves, minced
Dash of allspice
¼ Teaspoon thyme
½ Teaspoon paprika
2 Teaspoons worcestershire sauce
Salt and pepper, to taste

Soak bread crumbs in Madeira wine for about 15 minutes. Combine all ingredients in a large mixing bowl. Mix well (hands are the best). If the mixture seems too dry, add a little more dry red wine. If time allows, let the mixture set 45 minutes to an hour before shaping. Shape into an oblong loaf and place in a roasting pan. Bake at 375° for 1 to 1¼ hours. Remove from pan and place on a heated platter. Reserve the juices for tomato sauce mixture. To serve: slice and top with tomato sauce. Pass any extra sauce at table.

Mu Shu Pork

Mu Shu is the name of a tree found in northern China that bears beautiful yellow flowers. When the eggs in this dish are quickly cooked in a preheated wok, they puff up and blossom, resembling the Mu Shu flower. Vegetarians can leave out the pork and still have a flavorful dish.

This Chinese specialty has become a favorite of Americans in oriental restaurants; it is many dishes in one. Within the Mandarin pancake, each ingredient retains its own unique texture and the taste combination varies with each bite.

You could use Syrian pita bread with its built-in pocket to hold the stuffing, but the bread has a coarse and absorbent texture. I prefer to use the Mandarin pancakes which can be purchased from any Chinese market. A Mexican flour tortilla would also be a reasonable substitute.

½ Pound pork, cut into thin strips
1 Teaspoon soy sauce
¼ Teaspoon cornstarch
1 Tablespoon oil
½ Cup cooking oil
3 Eggs, whipped
½ Cup bamboo shoots
2 Large shitake mushrooms, cut into thin strips
2 Cups cabbage, shredded
2 Green onions, white part slivered, green tops chopped
2 Tablespoons soy sauce
½ Teaspoon sugar
¼ Teaspoon white peper
¼ Teaspoon sesame oil
½ Cup hoisin sauce
1 Teaspoon sesame oil
10 Mandarin pancakes, steamed 3-4 minutes, in towel

Combine pork with 1 teaspoon soy sauce, ¼ teaspoon cornstarch and 1 tablespoon oil. Mix well. Set aside to marinate for 30 minutes. Heat wok, or large heavy fry pan, over high heat. When hot, add ½ cup oil. When smoking, add eggs. Scramble until golden and set. Remove and drain. Add pork and cook until well done. Remove and drain. Remove all but 2 tablespoons of oil. Add mushrooms, bamboo shoots and pork. Stir-fry about 2 minutes. Add cabbage, green onion tops (reserve the white slivered parts), soy sauce, sugar, white pepper, and ¼ teaspoon sesame oil. Mix well. Add the drained eggs. Combine well. Transfer to a heated platter. Mix hoisin sauce with 1 teaspoon sesame oil. On a pancake, lightly spread some of the hoisin mixture and a few slivers of onion. Spoon 2 tablespoons of the pork mixture into the center of the pancake. Fold and serve.

Pork Loin Braised In Milk

Merle Ellis is responsible for me getting my start in television. He called to tell me of an opening for a "chef" position on "Evening Magazine", so I went to interview and audition for the 90 second spot on the show. I was selected and it was a lot of fun working with Jan Yanehiro. From there, I moved over to the "People Are Talking" show where I am in my seventh year.

Merle is a former television producer for NBC and has been involved in media communications for many years. He is still a practicing butcher in the town of Mill Valley, California, a syndicated newspaper columnist and author of the best selling book, "Cutting Up In The Kitchen".

When Merle came to the show as my guest chef, he brought with him a whole pork loin. He cut it up for us and we prepared this recipe that he had learned from the great Italian chef, Marcella Hazan.

2 Tablespoons butter, unsalted
2 Tablespoons vegetable oil
2 Pounds pork loin in one piece, with some fat on it, securely tied
1 Teaspoon salt
Freshly ground pepper, 3 or 4 twists of the mill
2½ Cups milk

Heat butter and oil over medium-high heat in a casserole large enough to contain pork. When butter foam subsides, add meat, fat side down. Brown thoroughly on all sides, lowering the heat if butter starts to turn dark brown. Add salt, pepper and milk. (Add milk slowly, otherwise it may boil over). Shortly after the milk comes to a boil, turn the heat down to medium, cover, with the lid partly askew, and cook slowly for about 1½ to 2 hours, until the meat is easily pierced by a fork. Turn and baste the meat from time to time, and, if necessary, add a little more milk. The milk will have coagulated into small nut-brown clusters. Remove the meat to a cutting board and allow to cool slightly for a few minutes. After removing the trussing string, carve into 3/8 inch slices and arrange on a warm platter. Draw off most of the fat and discard, being careful not to discard any of the coagulated milk clusters. Taste and correct for salt. Add 2-3 tablespoons of warm water; turn the heat to high, and boil away the water while scraping and loosening all the cooking residue in the pot. Spoon sauce over sliced pork and serve immediately.

Pork Tenderloin With Mustard Sauce

One of my favorite pork dishes is a pork tenderloin with this tangy mustard sauce. We have it at home at least once a month and each of us always looks forward to it.

Many people mistakenly believe that pork contains a lot of fat. Perhaps that was true many years ago, but not today. Today's pork contains 50% more lean meat than the pork of 30 years ago. With its high nutrient density, pork is an excellent food for a dieter. It is especially high in thiamin, protein, vitamin B and iron.

There are those who are still concerned about trichinosis. This disease is a medical rarity in the United States. For your piece of mind, however, remember all chance of the disease is eliminated if pork is cooked to 140° F.

Pork will take kindly to almost any treatment except fast cooking. In this recipe the chops are marinated in a sweet and sour sauce and then baked in a slow oven. To serve, thinly slice the meat and top with the rich and tangy sauce.

¼ Cup soy sauce
½ Cup dry white wine
4 Tablespoons brown sugar
3 Pork tenderloins, approximately 1 pound each
1 Tablespoon dry mustard
4 Tablespoons Dijon mustard
2 Tablespoons sugar
½ Teaspoon salt
2 Tablespoons vinegar
4 Egg yolks, beaten
1 Cup heavy cream
2 Hard-boiled eggs, finely chopped

Mix the soy sauce, wine and brown sugar together. Pour over the pork and marinate for 2-3 hours, turning a couple of times. Remove meat from marinade. Bake in a 350° oven for approximately 30 minutes or until the internal temperature is 140°. Meanwhile, put the dry mustard, Dijon mustard, sugar, salt, vinegar and beaten egg yolks into a heavy saucepan or a double boiler. Cook, stirring constantly, until thickened, about 8-10 minutes. Remove from heat. Cool. Add the cream and hard-boiled eggs. Blend.

Rack of Lamb With Garlic & Rosemary

My birthday is on the 6th of February, the same day as Ronald Reagan. In January, 1986, I wrote the White House and invited the President to come to the "People Are Talking" show as my guest on the cooking segment. I stated that I would prepare a special menu in honor of our birthdays and accompany it with some of my favorite California wines. This was my menu:

Shrimp Salad
Sterling Sauvignon Blanc

Rack of Lamb with Garlic & Rosemary
Stuffed Tomatoes
Potatoes Parisienne
Beaulieu Vineyards Cabernet Sauvignon

Cherry Tart

Well, the morning of the show, the White House called and President Reagan's press secretary said, "Mr. Reagan sends his regrets; he'll be unable to attend, but thank you for the invitation." We did the show without him and with the help of both Ann and Ross, we prepared the entire meal. Mary joined us on the set at the end of the show when we sat down to enjoy the meal and toast the "birthday boys".

2 Racks of lamb (6 chops each)
2 Cups of white wine
½ Cup olive oil
Fresh rosemary, several sprigs
6 Garlic cloves, mashed
Salt and pepper, to taste

Have the butcher thoroughly trim the racks for you. Place in a shallow baking dish. Mix white wine, olive oil and garlic together and pour over lamb. Add several sprigs of fresh rosemary. Marinate several hours or overnight in the refrigerator.

Remove the rack from the refrigerator 2 hours prior to roasting. Place in a roasting pan and season with salt and freshly ground pepper. Roast in a preheated 450° oven for 20-25 minutes.

Arrange on a serving platter. Garnish with additional rosemary sprigs and fresh garlic cloves. Serve at once.

Sauerbraten

Sauerbraten is beef that is marinated for a minimum of four days in spiced vinegar and wine, cooked and then served with a sweet and sour gravy.

It is common in every region of Germany but most famous is the Rhineland area. In other regions, the versions differ in the composition and seasonings of the gravy. In some recipes the sauce is enriched with raisins and sweetened with apples or corn syrup; I prefer the ginger snaps.

While stationed in Germany during my military tour of duty, I ate sauerbraten in every region I traveled and I always enjoyed it with a couple of steins of good, hearty German beer. When I prepare it at home, I accompany it with the beer and also some fabulous zucchini pancakes (page 204).

½ Cup burgundy wine
½ Cup red wine vinegar
2 Cups cold water
1 Onion, peeled and thinly sliced
5 Black peppercorns, coarsely crushed
4 Whole juniper berries, coarsely crushed
2 Bay leaves
4 Pounds boneless beef roast (bottom round or rump, trimmed)
½ Cup onions, finely chopped
½ Cup carrots, finely chopped
¼ Cup celery, finely chopped
2 Tablespoons flour
½ Cup water
½ Cup gingersnap crumbs
2 Tablespoons oil

In a 2-3 quart saucepan, combine the wine, vinegar, water, sliced onion, crushed peppercorns, juniper berries and bay leaves. Bring this marinade to a boil over high heat, then remove it from the heat and let it cool to room temperature. Place the beef in a deep crock or a deep stainless-steel or enamel pot just large enough to hold it comfortably. Pour the marinade over it. Cover the pan tightly for 4-5 days, turning the meat over at least twice a day.

Remove the meat from the marinade and pat it completely dry with paper towels. In a heavy pot, heat the oil over high heat. Add the meat and brown it on all sides. Transfer the meat to a platter. Add the chopped onions, carrots and celery to the fat and cook, stirring frequently, for 5-8 minutes. Sprinkle 2 tablespoons of flour over the vegetables, stirring constantly. Pour in 2 cups of the reserved marinade and ½ cup of water. Bring to a boil over high heat. Return the meat to the pot. Cover tightly and simmer for at least 2 hours. Transfer the meat to a heated platter and cover with foil.

Skim any fat from the surface and add 1 cup of the reserved marinade and the gingersnaps. The crumbs will disintegrate in the sauce and thicken it slightly. Strain. Return the sauce to the pan, taste for seasonings and let simmer over low heat until ready to serve. To serve, carve in ¼ inch slices and arrange on a heated platter. Spoon a bit of the sauce over the slices. Pour the remaining sauce in a small pitcher and pass at the table.

Short Ribs In Beer

Short Ribs in Beer, a traditional Belgian dish, is relatively inexpensive and contains three basic ingredients: beef, onions and beer.

Out of the pot, after cooking, comes a dish that is neither harsh nor heavy, but lightly and pleasantly flavored. As happens when liquor is used in cooking, the alcohol in the beer evaporates but the flavor remains, in this case, to give a suggestion of sweetness.

This is a fine entree to serve on a cold winter night. When the lid of the pot is lifted, an aroma wafts across the table that will tempt any appetite. I like to serve it with some steamed carrots that have been glazed with butter and a bit of sugar, some boiled potatoes and a frosty, cold beer.

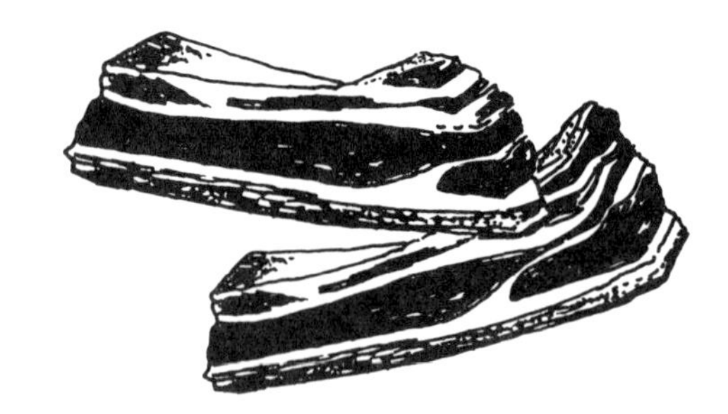

4-5 Pounds lean beef short ribs
½ Cup flour
½ Cup vegetable oil
6 Large yellow onions, sliced
4 Garlic cloves, crushed
½ Cup parsley, freshly chopped
Salt and pepper, to taste
2 Teaspoons dried thyme
¼ Cup brown sugar
¼ Cup red wine vinegar
1 10½ ounce can beef broth
3 12 ounce cans of beer

Cut beef ribs into 2" x 2" pieces. Flour lightly and brown a few at a time in hot vegetable oil. Place into a large oven-proof casserole. Preheat oven to 300°. Add onions to oil and saute gently. Add garlic, chopped parsley, salt, pepper, thyme, brown sugar and vinegar. Pour in broth and heat to boiling. Pour over meat. Add beer and cover casserole. Bake in oven for 2-2½ hours until meat is tender. Remove ribs to a warm platter. Skim any grease from top of the sauce. Taste and adjust the seasonings. If necessary, thicken sauce by boiling and reducing. To serve, pour sauce over ribs and serve at once.

Veal Picatta

Veal, young beef three to eight months of age, has a superbly delicate and distinctive flavor. The very best, milk-fed veal, should be tender and succulent and have a white or very pale pink color. The redder the meat, the older and tougher the veal.

When preparing this recipe, ask your friendly butcher for veal scaloppine. Once cut, the scaloppine must be pounded flat, being careful not to break it up or pound holes in it. You want to stretch the meat from the center outward until it is evenly thinned.

This veal entree with its zesty, lemon-caper sauce is best served with Potatoes Parisienne (page 196).

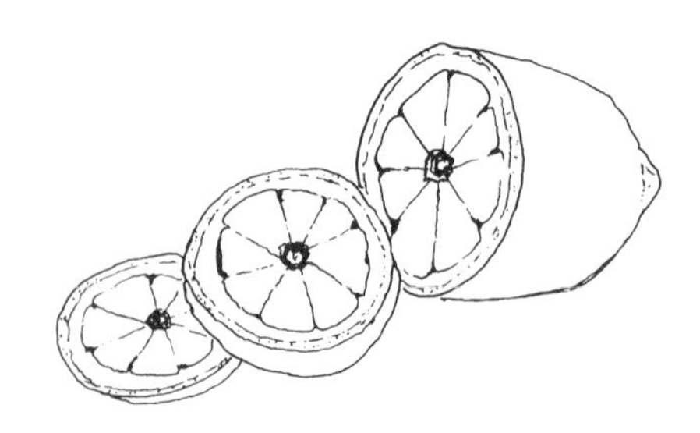

4 Veal scallops (¼ inch thick)
Salt and pepper, to taste
Flour
4 Tablespoons butter
2 Tablespoons lemon juice, freshly squeezed
2 Tablespoons capers
1 Tablespoon parsley, freshly chopped
½ Cup dry white wine

Season the veal with salt and pepper and dust lightly with flour. Melt 3 tablespoons of the butter in a large skillet and brown the meat over high heat for a minute and a half on each side. Transfer the meat to a warmed platter. Mix the remaining butter and the wine with the meat juices in the pan and cook over high heat until the butter takes on a pale brown color. Add the lemon juice and capers. Heat thoroughly. Pour the sauce over the veal. Sprinkle with the chopped parsley and serve immediately. Serves: 2.

Veal Madeleine

One day Mary spent the afternoon at the beauty shop getting a permanent (so I'm giving away family secrets...she doesn't have naturally curly hair!). We hadn't discussed dinner plans beforehand as we usually do, so it was up to me to choose the entree at the butcher shop. I chose a veal steak, not realizing that it is not too high on Mary's list of favorites.

Now the payoff of this story could be that the veal steak was fixed so deliciously that she went into ecstasies over it. Well, that is exactly what happened! So the moral of the story is, if you think you do not like veal, try this recipe. It is a thick veal steak, pan-browned, smothered with golden brown onions, simmered in wine, and set on a bed of noodles which have been paprika'd, buttered, sprinkled with almonds, and served with a sour cream, herb, and sherry sauce.

1 Veal steak, 1¼ inches thick
¼ Cup flour
1 Tablespoon paprika
1 Teaspoon salt
3 Tablespoons bacon drippings (or olive oil)
3 Medium onions
1 Cup sour cream
2 Tablespoons dry sherry
½ Teaspoon dried oregano
Cooked noodles
Butter
Slivered almonds
Sliced stuffed olives

Combine the flour, paprika, and salt. Dredge the veal steak thoroughly with this mixture.

In the bacon drippings (or olive oil) in a heavy skillet saute the onions, sliced thin, over low heat until they are soft and golden brown, then remove them from the skillet. Brown the floured veal steak well on both sides in the same skillet. When browned, place the sauteed onions on top of the veal steak in the skillet. Add any remaining seasoned flour mixture to the skillet along with the wine. Cover and simmer until the veal is tender, about 45 minutes. Remove veal and onions to a heated platter.

To make the gravy, add the sour cream, dry sherry, and oregano to the skillet juices. Stir and blend thoroughly and heat to serving temperature. Surround the veal and onions with cooked noodles which have been buttered and sprinkled with paprika and slivered almonds. Garnish with sliced stuffed olives. Serve the gravy separately.

TRUCK
2
SFFD

SEAFOOD

Blackened Redfish

Probably the most popular recipe that Louisianna chef Paul Prudhomme has introduced to this country is his blackened redfish. In his first video*, he shows how to prepare this recipe to perfection with some helpful tips.

Redfish is not readily available here on the west coast, so I use red snapper, which is a perfect substitute. This recipe also works well with salmon steaks or filets. In either case, the filets or steaks should not be more than ¾ inch thick.

Cooking the fish in your kitchen will smoke up the entire room, trust me, I know! I suggest that this be done outside on the bar-b-que. Prepare a hot fire of briquets in a mound. Heat your cast iron skillet on the stove in the house for at least 10 minutes. With several hot pads and a clear path, rush the skillet to the bar-b-que. Close the door behind you and cook the fish as directed.

Combined with Seafood Dirty Rice (page 274), you will have a perfect Cajun dinner.

*Paul's video can be found at most local video stores. I recommend it as one of the best cooking videos around. In San Francisco, there is a store that specializes in cookbooks and cooking videos. It is called "Gourmet Guides" (See Appendix).

¾ Pound unsalted butter, melted in a skillet
1 Tablespoon sweet paprika
2½ Teaspoons salt
1 Teaspoon onion powder
1 Teaspoon garlic powder
1 Teaspoon ground red pepper (preferably cayenne)
¾ Teaspoon white pepper
¾ Teaspoon black pepper
½ Teaspoon dried thyme leaves
½ Teaspoon dried oregano leaves
6 8-10 ounce fish filets (preferably redfish, pompano or tilefish), cut about ½ inch thick

Heat a large cast-iron skillet over very high heat until it is beyond the smoking stage and you can see white ash in the skillet bottom (the skillet cannot be too hot for this dish), at least 10 minutes. Meanwhile, pour 2 tablespoons melted butter in each of 6 small ramekins; set aside and keep warm. Reserve the remaining butter in its skillet. Heat the serving plates in a 250° oven. Thoroughly combine the seasoning mix ingredients in a small bowl. Dip each filet in the reserved melted butter so that both sides are well coated. Then sprinkle seasoning mix generously and evenly on both sides, patting it in by hand. Place in the hot skillet and pour 1 teaspoon of melted butter on top of each filet. Be careful, as the butter may flame up. Cook, uncovered, over the same high heat until the underside looks charred, about 2 minutes. The time will vary according to the thickness of the filet and the heat of the skillet. Turn the fish over and again pour 1 teaspoon of melted butter on top. Cook until fish is done, about 2 minutes more. Serve each filet while piping hot with a ramekin of butter on each plate.

Blackened Swordfish with Chardonnay and Lime Butter

To celebrate the one hundredth birthday of the Statue of Liberty, J.C. Penney asked a diverse group of celebrities to contribute a favorite recipe to their "Salute to America Celebrity" cookbook. In September, 1986, I featured the book on my cooking segment. Each of the fifty states is represented by a celebrity. I picked Georgia and invited Burt Reynolds to be my guest chef. He couldn't make it; as a matter of fact he didn't even return my call, so I prepared the recipe without him!

In the cookbook Burt mentions that not everyone marinates fish when it is to be blackened, but he believes this is the only way for the dish to be prepared.

Chardonnay is a rather expensive wine to use for marinating. I personally think that chablis could be substituted without any noticeable difference.

2 8 ounce swordfish filets

Marinade:

4 Tablespoons olive oil
1 Tablespoon wine vinegar
1/8 Cup chardonnay wine
1/2 Teaspoon coarse salt
2 Garlic cloves, minced

Lime Butter: *(enough for 8 filets)

1 Cup whipped butter
2 Limes, juice and zest
1 Teaspoon sugar
1 Teaspoon salt
1/2 Teaspoon pepper
1/8 Cup chardonnay wine

Blackened Seasoning:

1½ Teaspoons oregano
1½ Teaspoons thyme
1½ Teaspoons marjoram
½ Teaspoon cayenne pepper
1 Teaspoon black pepper
½ Teaspoon salt

Marinate fish for 1 hour. Coat fish with blackened seasoning. Get a large, cast iron skillet very hot and lay the seasoned fish inside. There will be enough oil in the marinade that the fish won't stick. After 5 minutes, check with your finger to see if flesh is firm. Turn filet over and cook for an additional 1-2 minutes. Do not overcook. Top with lime butter and a twist of fresh lime.

*When making the lime butter, to get the butter to blend with the lime juice and wine, add 2 tablespoons of fresh, unseasoned bread crumbs.

Burmese Curry Fish

Burma is located between India and Thailand and therefore shares culinary preferences with both areas. Their curries resemble those of India and their fish sauces and pastes are almost identical to those in Thailand. The Burmese dislike the coconut oil of India and prefer to cook with either sesame or peanut oil. As they use fewer aromatic herbs, their curry sauces tend to be sweet and less smooth, although they are just as spicy hot as those of Thailand.

Some of my favorite Burmese dishes are their crisp and refreshing salads which are heavily spiced with garlic, ginger, scallions and tiny chilies.

Although the recipe specifically calls for catfish, any firm white fish would be a good substitute. The owner, Phil Chu, also prepares this recipe with fresh salmon.

Jim's Featured Pick:

NAN YANG
301 8th Street
Oakland, CA
(415) 465-6924

¼ Cup peanut oil
1 Large onion, chopped
4 Garlic cloves, minced
1 Tablespoon fresh ginger, minced
1 Stock lemon grass,* halved
1½ Tablespoons curry powder
1 Teaspoon cumin powder
¼ Teaspoon chili powder
½ Teaspoon paprika powder
6 Catfish filets, 1½ inches thick
1 Cup water
2 Tomatoes, cut in wedges
1 Teaspoon tamarind powder*
2 Tablespoons fresh cilantro, chopped
Whole cilantro sprigs for garnish

In skillet, heat oil. Add onion and garlic and saute briefly. Add ginger, lemon grass, curry, cumin, chili powder and paprika. Reduce heat and cook 2 minutes, using caution as to not let the curry burn. Add fish filets and saute an additional 1 minute. Add water, tomatoes (salt may be added according to personal taste), tamarind powder and chopped cilantro. Cover and simmer 4-5 minutes, until fish flakes easily with fork. Garnish with fresh cilantro sprigs. Serve with steamed rice.

*Available at Chinese markets in San Francisco and Oakland.

Chilean Sea Bass

When dining out, Mary and I look for a restaurant which offers a variety of moderately priced entrees, a selective and affordable wine list and a quiet, friendly setting. All of this is available at the "Sea Chanteys" restaurant on Van Ness in San Francisco; it is tastefully luxurious, but without ostentation. Owner and chef Mark Zehdl welcomes you with a smile that is definitely Old World, as is his meticulous attention to your food and service.

Mark does all the buying himself and insists on the freshest of ingredients. He picks up his seafood daily from local fish mongers or at San Francisco International Airport from as far away as the East Coast, the South Seas, the great Northwest or South America.

Jim's Featured Pick:

SEA CHANTEY
1233 Van Ness Avenue
San Francisco, CA
(415) 673-0558

2 Boneless bass filets
Salt
White pepper
Flour
2 Tablespoons oil
1 Cup shitake mushrooms, sliced
2 Tablespoons parsley, freshly chopped
1 Garlic clove, minced
½ Cup Amontillado sherry*
2 Tablespoons butter

Season fish with salt and pepper. Dredge in flour. Shake off excess. Heat oil to hot in a saute pan. Add fish. Cook briefly, approximately 1-2 minutes per side, depending on the thickness of the filets. Do not overcook. Remove fish to a heated platter. Drain oil from pan. Return pan to heat. Add butter, mushrooms, parsley, garlic and sherry. Cook about 1 minute. Pour over top of filets. Serve at once. Serves: 2.

*Dry Spanish sherry

Coquilles St. Jacques

Scallops are familiar to nearly everyone because of their beautiful symmetrical shells whose shape has fascinated artists for hundreds of years. The shells are also used as baking dishes in thousands of homes, indeed, the cooking term "to scallop" originally meant cooked in scallop shells.

Although found on both American coasts, the commercial catch of scallops is practically all from the Atlantic; Pacific scallops being few and far between. The tiny bay scallops of inshore waters are seldom seen in the market, most of them going to supply the restaurant trade. They are worth seeking out, however, as they are tender and delicate in flavor.

In this country, only the central muscle which controls the shell movement is eaten. Unlike oysters and clams which move about slowly by means of an extruded "foot," scallops propel themselves by opening their shells, then rapidly closing them - a sort of primitive jet propulsion.

Scallops are sold shelled and trimmed, fresh, frozen or breaded and frozen. They are extremely succulent, the meat resembling crab meat in texture and flavor. Like other shellfish, care must be taken not to overcook them, for they become tough and stringy.

Jim's Featured Pick:

BEAU RIVAGE
1042 Ballena Boulevard
Alameda, CA 94501
(415) 523-1660

12 Scallops
Salt and pepper
Flour
2-3 Tablespoons oil
2 Tablespoons butter
4 Large mushrooms, chopped
2 Small shallots
1 Garlic clove, crushed
¼ Cup dry white wine
Fresh parsley, chopped

Lightly salt and pepper the scallops. Dust with flour and shake off any excess. Heat oil in saute pan until hot. Add scallops and cook about 1 minute on each side. DO NOT OVERCOOK. Remove to a heated platter and keep warm. Drain oil. Add butter, mushrooms, shallots, garlic and wine to saute pan. Cook about 1-2 minutes, or until the butter is melted and the sauce thickens. Return scallops to skillet for about 1 minute. Add freshly chopped parsley and serve immediately. Serves: 2.

Crab Legs Saute

This recipe is one that Mary and I reserve for just the two of us. It is a meal that we can prepare in just a short time when we arrive home late in the afternoon from work. Mary will wash and dry some assorted salad greens and make a vinaigrette dressing. I'll steam some rice to accompany the crab legs. While doing our prep work in the kitchen, we will share a glass of wine and discuss the day's events.

The crab must be fresh and since it is already cooked, it only need be heated through; overcooking will make it mushy. Since crab legs can be a bit expensive, I recommend preparing this recipe for an intimate dinner for two.

2 Tablespoons sweet butter
1 Garlic clove, mashed
1 Small onion, finely chopped
2 Tablespoons parsley, freshly chopped
1 Tablespoon lemon juice, freshly squeezed
½ Cup dry white wine
Salt and pepper, to taste
10 Whole crab legs

In a heavy skillet, melt butter. Add garlic and gently saute the garlic to flavor the butter (Do not let the garlic burn in the butter). Remove the garlic. Add the onion and saute gently for 3-5 minutes. Add the parsley, white wine and lemon juice. Season with salt and pepper. Cook for approximately 4-5 minutes or until the sauce thickens slightly. Add the crab legs and heat through. Serve at once.

Fish Filets with Cucumber Sauce

This is a recipe I featured during January, my traditional "Diet Month." It is a one-dish-meal which is low in calories, nutritious, delicious and very pleasing to the eye. It consists of a boneless poached fish filet served on a bed of spinach and topped with a wonderful cucumber yogurt sauce.

I prefer to use a firm, white fleshed fish such as a snapper or rock cod. I do not recommend using filet of sole or butter fish.

Tip: When preparing the fish, I first rinse the filets well and pat dry with a paper towel. Then, with my index finger, I feel for any bones and remove them with a clean pair of pliers.

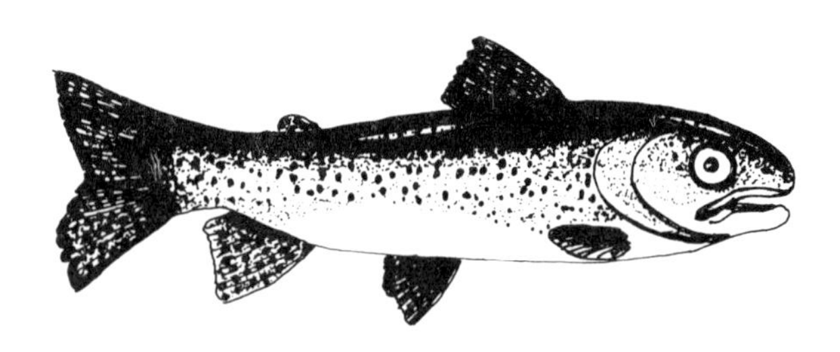

4 Boneless fish filets
Salt and pepper, to taste
Dash of cayenne (optional)
4 Sprigs fresh dill
¼ Cup dry white wine
3 Bunches fresh spinach, cleaned and chopped

Season fish with salt, pepper and dash of cayenne. Place a sprig of dill in center of each filet. Roll filet and place in a shallow baking dish. Add wine. Cover with foil and bake in a 350° oven for 15-20 minutes. Cook spinach, covered, for 7 minutes or less. Drain. Squeeze dry. Put back into pot to keep warm.

Sauce

1 Cucumber
2 Tablespoons onion, finely chopped
Juice of ½ lemon
1 Tablespoon dill, freshly chopped
Dash of tabasco (optional)
½ Cup plain yogurt
½ Cup imitation sour cream
Salt and pepper, to taste

Wash, seed and coarsely chop cucumber. Combine with onion, lemon juice, chopped dill, tabasco, yogurt, sour cream, salt and pepper. Blend well.

To serve: Divide spinach into four portions and arrange on individual serving plates. Place a rolled fish filet on top. Spoon cucumber sauce over filet. Garnish with a sprig of fresh dill. Pass extra sauce.

Fish Pie

Every year around St. Patrick's Day, I like to prepare a traditional Irish dish on the show. In March, 1986, I featured this recipe for fish pie.

The traditional Irish are inclined to cling to the past and its local recipes. They eat a lot of fish and potatoes because a lot of fish and potatoes are available in Ireland. They have a variety of fresh seafood to choose from: mackeral, cod, salmon, lobster, prawns and dover sole, just to name a few. The Irish have been growing potatoes since the 17th century when some were brought to Ireland from the new world.

This one dish meal is easy to prepare, nutritious, economical and a wonderful tribute to Ireland.

4 Ounces butter
2 Onions, sliced
4 Tablespoons flour
1 ¾ Cups milk
¼ Cup chopped parsley
1 Tablespoon anchovy paste
Dash of cayenne
½ Teaspoon fennel seeds

Any combination of four of the fish listed below:

2 Rock cod or snapper filets
2 Salmon steaks, boned and skinned
½ Pound scallops
¼ Pound shrimp
½ Pound fresh crab meat
6 Jumbo prawns, peeled and deveined

6 Medium potatoes, cooked and mashed
¼ Cup of milk
4 Tablespoons butter

Melt 4 ounces of butter in medium sauce pan. Add onions. Saute until soft, 3-5 minutes. Add flour and mix well. Stir in 1 ¾ cups milk and bring to a boil. Stir until smooth. Remove from heat. Mix in parsley, anchovy paste, cayenne pepper and fennel seeds. Cut fish in serving size pieces and add seafood to sauce. Place in 4-5 quart casserole. Mix mashed potatoes with ¼ cup milk and 2 tablespoons melted butter. Cover seafood mixture with mashed potatoes. Dot with additional 2 tablespoons butter. Bake in a preheated 375° oven for 30 minutes. Place under broiler for 5 minutes to brown.

Grilled Fish with Garlic Beurre Rouge

It is always exciting to attend the Gilroy Garlic Festival which is held the last weekend in July. I have attended the last five festivals either as a judge, master of ceremonies, guest chef or as an observer. It is wonderful to be in the kitchens at the fair grounds when all the pots and pans are sending out grand odors of cooking garlic. In 1984, over 900 recipes were submitted for the garlic recipe cook-off from all across the United States. Preliminary screening reduces the finalists to twelve amateur chefs and they must attend the festival and prepare their recipes for a panel of six judges. The final cook-off takes a couple of hours and quite a crowd gathers. Some of the finalists even bring their own rooting sections. As a judge, I always bring a hearty appetite and some breath mints!

This recipe won first prize at the 6th Annual Festival in 1984 and was submitted by Mrs. Beverly Stone of Berkeley, California.

½ Cup fruity olive oil
5 Tablespoons lemon juice, freshly squeezed
4 Garlic cloves, peeled and slivered
1 Bunch cilantro, chopped to make ½ cup, reserving some whole leaves for garnish
Salt and freshly ground pepper, to taste
6 6 ounce firm fleshed fish filets, about ¾ inch thick
¼ Pound butter, unsalted
¼ Cup red onion, chopped
2 Small hot green chilies, finely minced
1 Tablespoon garlic, freshly minced
1 Pound ripe tomatoes, peeled and chopped
Lemon wedges

Mix together olive oil, 4 tablespoons lemon juice, slivered garlic, ¼ cup chopped cilantro, salt and pepper. Add fish filets and marinate for a minimum of 1 hour.

Meanwhile prepare Garlic Beurre Rouge. In a frying pan, over medium heat, melt 2 tablespoons butter. Saute onion, chilies and minced garlic until soft, stirring often. Add tomatoes and the remaining 1 tablespoon lemon juice. Cook for 10 minutes, stirring occasionally. Remove from heat. Salt and pepper, to taste. Stir in the remaining ¼ cup cilantro. Slowly stir in the remaining butter until melted.

Barbecue the fish over low glowing coals, about 7 minutes or until done to your preference, turning the fish only once. Remove to a warmed serving platter. Top with the garlic beurre rouge sauce. Garnish with lemon wedges and reserved whole cilantro leaves. Serves: 6.

Paella

It is said if you ask one hundred average men in Spain what goes into Paella, you will get three hundred answers, giving one from himself, one from his mother and one from his wife! Obviously, the dish draws upon a variety of possible ingredients: lobster, shrimp, clams, mussels, squid, sausage, chicken, rabbit, string beans, peas and red peppers. Only olive oil, rice and saffron are always used.

Paella is not difficult to prepare and requires no special equipment other than a large, deep, flat bottom skillet or roasting pan. The name "paella" originates from the utensil in which the dish is cooked. The Spanish word for skillet is "paella." It is quite large as this is a dish usually prepared for many. Paella pans are available at your local gourmet shop.

Paella is one of those rare dishes that gets better and better as you eat it because when the rice is cooked with certain other foods it absorbs and combines all the flavors until it has a unique special flavor of its own.

8 Medium prawns
8 Clams
8 Mussels
4 Hot Italian sausages
1 Whole chicken, cut into serving pieces
½ Cup olive oil
Salt and pepper, to taste
1 Cup boneless pork or ham, cubed
2 Garlic cloves, crushed
1 Large yellow onion, chopped
1 Red or green pepper, seeded and cut into strips
2 Tomatoes, peeled, seeded and chopped
3 Cups of rice
¼ Teaspoon saffron
6 Cups chicken broth
1 Package frozen peas

Peel and devein the prawns. Scrub mussels and clams thoroughly. Set aside. Prick the sausages with the tip of a knife. Place in skillet and cover with water and bring to a boil. Reduce and simmer, uncovered about 10 minutes. Drain and slice into ¼ inch rounds. Season chicken with salt and pepper. Heat ¼ cup of olive oil in heavy skillet. Brown chicken pieces slowly, turning occasionally. Cook until evenly colored. Remove and place on a paper towel to absorb any extra oil. Drain skillet and wipe dry. Add another ¼ cup of olive oil. Heat until hot. Add pork or ham. Stir and cook 1-2 minutes. Add garlic, onion, pepper and tomatoes. Saute until mixture softens. In a paella pan or oven proof casserole, combine the rice, onion-pepper mixture and saffron. Add the chicken broth. Bring to a boil on top of the stove. Remove from heat. Arrange the chicken, prawns, clams, mussels and sausage in casserole. Scatter peas on top. Cover. Bake in a preheated 400° oven for 45 minutes or unti rice is done and has absorbed all of the liquid. Do not stir while in the oven. Remove from oven and serve at once. Serves: 8.

Salmon with Pepper Sauces

This recipe may be prepared with either red or green peppers. I prepare it with both and make a red pepper sauce and a green pepper sauce.

The peppers may be peeled with a paring knife or a vegetable peeler. I prefer to roast them whole under a hot broiler. When the skin is completely blackened, after turning several times, I place them under a damp towel for 20 minutes. This will cause them to steam and the skins will peel easily.

To serve, I place the cooked salmon on a heated dinner plate and ladle a bit of the red sauce on one side and a bit of the green sauce on the other. I top it with a sprig of fresh dill and serve it at once. The presentation is beautiful!

Because of the sauces on the dinner plate, I usually accompany this entree with a vegetable on the side, such as a plate of fresh asparagus or a steamed artichoke, whichever happens to be in season at the time.

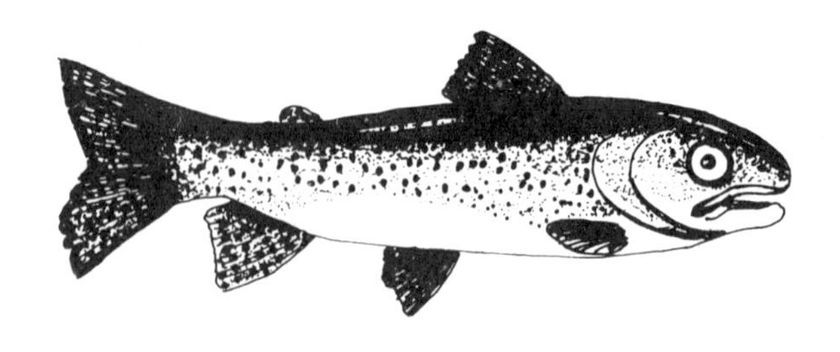

2 Bell peppers (red or green)
2 Small shallots, finely chopped
3 Tablespoons butter, unsalted
½ Cup heavy cream
Salt and white pepper, to taste
Fresh dill

Peel peppers. Remove seeds and chop coarsely. Saute shallots in 2 tablespoons of the butter 2-3 minutes. (A small yellow onion may be substituted.) Add peppers and continue cooking 2-3 minutes more. Remove from heat and puree in blender or food processor. Return to a small saucepan. Add cream and remaining 1 tablespoon butter. Season with salt and pepper. Heat and serve.

Poach salmon filets in ½ inch of equal parts water and a dry white wine. Depending on the thickness of the filets, the poaching process should be less than 10 minutes.

Salmon in Parchment

Salmon cooked in parchment is probably one of the most delectable dishes in the realm of fish cookery. In the first place, salmon with its rich, delicately flavored flesh, is considered to be one of the choicest of salt water fishes. And the cooking of it in a sealed paper bag, covered with a sauce, only enhances its flavor. The Metropole Restaurant in Berkeley, California, operated by chef and owner Serge Bled, in his high culinary tradition, prepares this recipe to perfection.

The story is told that a famous balloonist who did stunts during the French army maneuvers was to be the entertainment at ''Antoines'' restaurant in New Orleans. The chef was told to prepare a dish which would resemble the gas envelope of a high rise balloon. So he set to work with a pair of scissors and cut some large hearts from parchment paper. Then he placed fish filets on the parchment hearts, spooned some sauce over them, sealed the bags and baked them in the oven. When the paper was brown, the entree was brought to the table, split open and eaten with gusto and much acclaim!

Jim's Featured Pick:

METROPOLE
2271 Shattuck Avenue
Berkeley, California
(415) 848-3080

2 6 ounce salmon filets
¼ Cup dry white wine
2 Tablespoons shallots, finely minced
Juice of ½ lemon
2 Tablespoons cilantro, freshly chopped
¼ Large red bell pepper, finely chopped
1 Large tomato, peeled, seeded and finely chopped
2 Green onions, finely chopped
2 Small sweet gherkins, finely chopped
12 Green peppercorns
Butter
Salt and pepper, to taste

Place filets in baking dish. Cover with white wine, shallots, lemon juice and 1 tablespoon of chopped cilantro. Set aside. Marinate for a minimum of 1 hour. In a small bowl, mix one tablespoon of chopped cilantro, red bell pepper, tomato, green onions, gherkins and peppercorns. Set aside. (Up to this point may be done in advance.) Approximately 20 minutes before you plan to serve dinner, cut 2 parchment paper hearts 8 inches long and 12 inches wide. Butter each piece of paper well and lay a salmon filet on one side of the heart. Cover with the relish mixture, salt and pepper to taste and a dab of butter. Fold the heart over and hand seal the edges. Place on a baking sheet and bake in a preheated 450° oven for 10-12 minutes. To serve, present each "package" to your guest and open at the table. Garnish with a lemon wedge and sprigs of fresh cilantro. Serves: 2.

Sauteed Crawfish

This is another recipe from the Louisiana kitchen of Paul Prudhomme. He has been a guest on the show several times and always delights us with his conversation and humor. (see photo, p. xiii)

Paul travels with a troupe of 4 or 5 chefs when coming to California. During the show, his chefs are in the KPIX employees' lunchroom cooking up some surprises! One time it was sweet potato omelets, the next time it was jambalaya. Paul says this is his way of showing "Southern Hospitality."

Paul recommends that the sauce for this dish be made only three servings at a time. If you want to make more than three servings, do so in separate batches, but always serve piping hot.

Crawfish are available frozen at most local supermarkets. Fresh crawfish, however, may be found at Safeway's Bon Appetit Markets and the Great Atlantic Seafood Company in Oakland.

1 Cup butter, unsalted
½ Cup green onions, tops only, finely chopped
1 Teaspoon garlic, minced
1 Pound peeled crawfish tails
1 Teaspoon tabasco sauce
Seasoning mix
½ Cup seafood stock or clam broth
1½ Cups hot cooked rice

Place ½ cup of the butter, onions and garlic in a large deep skillet. Saute 1 minute over high heat; turn off heat. Add the crawfish, tabasco and seasoning mix. Turn heat to high and saute about 3 minutes, stirring occasionally. Add the remaining ½ cup of butter, breaking it into chunks in the pan; then slowly add the stock while moving the pan back and forth on the burner. Shake the pan hard enough to toss, but not spill the ingredients. Cook over high heat 6 minutes, shaking the pan constantly. To serve: mound ½ cup rice in the middle of each serving plate. Encircle the rice with 1 cup of the sauteed crawfish and their sauce. Serves: 3.

Seasoning Mix

1 Teaspoon white pepper
½ Teaspoon salt
½ Teaspoon ground red pepper, preferably cayenne
½ Teaspoon black pepper
½ Teaspoon dried sweet basil leaves
¼ Teaspoon dry mustard

TRUCK
2
S.F.F.D

POULTRY

Buttermilk Fried Chicken

Question: "What is the All-American picnic favorite?"

Answer: "Fried Chicken."

Various parts of the country have their own traditional methods of preparing fried chicken. The best I have ever tasted comes from Jeanne Parent of Healdsburg, California. She won first prize in the 1986 Sonoma-Marin County Fair. I helped judge the contest and I can honestly say that it was unanimous among the judges that this recipe deserved the blue ribbon.

The success of deep frying depends on the temperature of the oil. It must be hot enough to make its action rapid and immediate. "Hot enough" means that the oil or fat must reach a temperature of at least 350°. A simple way to gauge the temperature is to drop a small piece of bread into the oil and if it turns golden brown in 1 minute, the oil has reached 350°. I prefer to take the temperature of the oil more accurately with a deep-frying thermometer clipped to the side of the pan.

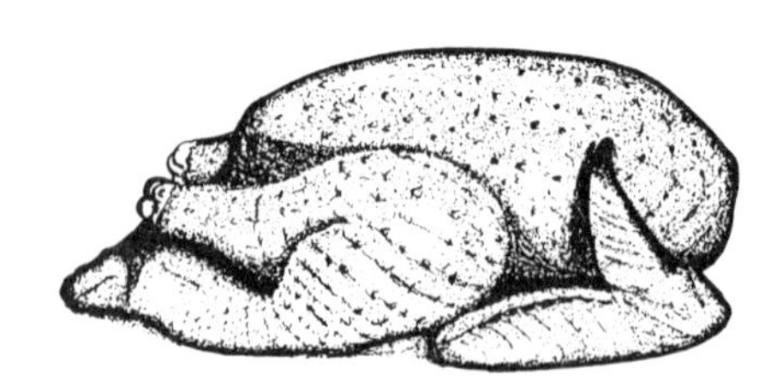

1 3 pound chicken, cut up
1½ Cups white flour
½ Cup bread crumbs, unseasoned
2½ Cups corn flakes, crushed to medium-fine
1 Teaspoon salt
½ Teaspoon pepper
½ Teaspoon garlic powder
1 Teaspoon poultry seasoning
½ Teaspoon paprika
2 Eggs
1 Cup buttermilk
2 Cups vegetable oil

Pat dry cut up pieces of chicken. Dust with ½ cup of flour. Set aside. In a small bowl, beat egg and buttermilk. In a large bowl, mix together all dry ingredients and spices. Place pieces of chicken, one at a time, into the buttermilk/egg mixture, then into the dry mixture. Meanwhile, heat 2 cups vegetable oil in heavy skillet. Fry chicken at medium high heat for 20-25 minutes, turning occasionally as it cooks to a golden brown.

Chicken Casserole Sabriye's Style

Our friend, Weezie Mott, teaches private cooking lessons and specializes in Italian and Middle Eastern Cuisine. Whenever I have a technical food question, need to borrow a special pot or pan, or just to share a glass of wine and talk recipes, I hop in the car and go visit Weezie. She only lives a few blocks away and always makes me feel like a special guest when I visit her home.

Her husband, Howard, worked for the American government and they lived, for several years, in Southern Italy as well as three years in Turkey. Weezie became dear friends with her neighbor, Sabriye, while living in Ankara, the capital. This recipe is from her and is so named, Chicken Casserole Sabriye's Style.

This one pot dinner is a wonderful combination of chicken stewed with garden fresh vegetables to an almost soup-like consistency. Served with a loaf of sourdough French bread and some white wine, it is a most pleasurable and remembered meal.

- **4 Large chicken breasts, boned and halved**
- **8 Tablespoons butter**
- **4 Tablespoons olive oil**
- **½ Pound green beans, whole**
- **1 Eggplant, cubed**
- **½ Pound okra, whole**
- **1 Yellow onion, coarsely chopped**
- **2 Green peppers, seeded and sliced**
- **3 Fresh tomatoes, peeled, seeded and sliced**
- **2 Medium zucchini, cut into ½" slices**
- **Salt, to taste**
- **White pepper, to taste**
- **1 Chicken bouillon cube**

Place 4 tablespoons butter in a saute pan and lightly saute the chicken breasts on both sides. Arrange the chicken on bottom of a casserole or dutch oven. Add olive oil to the saute pan. Add eggplant and saute for a few minutes on each side. Remove with a slotted spoon and arrange over the chicken. Follow same procedure with onions, peppers and zucchini. Add a bit of salt, freshly ground white pepper and half of a pulverized chicken bouillon cube. Blanch the green beans in boiling water for one minute. Drain well. Place them over the sauteed vegetables. Arrange okra on top of green beans and place tomato slices over the okra. Add additional salt, pepper and remainder of the chicken bouillon cube plus thin slices of butter. Cover and bake in a 350° oven for 45 minutes. Remove the cover and bake for additional 15 minutes. Note: If the pan juices seem too watery, pour them off into a small pan and boil them down rapidly on top of the stove. Pour the thickened juices over the vegetables in the casserole. Serve immediately.

Chicken Cordon Bleu

Presented in different ways, boned and stuffed chicken breasts are featured in many cuisines. The most celebrated are the Russian dish called "Chicken Kiev," the French dish called "Chicken Cordon Bleu" and the Italian dish called "Saltimbocca."

When you want to stuff chicken breasts, you not only skin and bone them, you also enlarge and flatten them so that you can fold the meat around the stuffing. The flattening should be gentle, but firm. I like to prepare the breasts at least a couple of hours in advance; letting them set gives the breading a chance to firm up and it adheres better during the cooking process.

If the chicken breasts are cooked in butter only, they will brown too quickly and burn. With the addition of a bit of oil, the burning point is considerably lower and they can cook for a longer period.

I recommend you prepare one breast per person and top with a rich, creamy onion sauce (page 57).

6 Half chicken breasts, boned and skinned
6 Boiled ham slices
6 Slices of cheese (Swiss or Monterey Jack) 2"x½"
Dijon mustard
Flour
2 Eggs, whipped
3 Cups fresh breadcrumbs
2 Tablespoons butter
2 Tablespoons olive oil

Filet chicken breasts. Place each breast between 2 sheets of plastic wrap and flatten to ¼ inch thickness. Top each breast with a slice of ham and a piece of cheese. Dab with a teaspoon of Dijon mustard. Roll chicken breast and pinch edges tightly. Dust with flour. Shake off excess. Dip into whipped eggs and coat with fresh bread crumbs. Place on a plate, cover and chill until ready to use. Melt butter and olive oil in a saute pan over medium heat. Brown chicken evenly on all sides. Total cooking time about 6 minutes. Place in a casserole dish. Cover with foil and bake in a preheated 375° oven for 15 minutes. Remove from oven and serve at once with onion cream sauce.

Chicken Crepes

This is the perfect casserole to prepare for your family; it is easy, economical and very tasty. It can also be made ahead of time and frozen, if necessary.

When I make crepes, I always make a double batch. I freeze the extras in packets of 6 or 8 and use them later with a variety of fresh fruit fillings as a last minute dessert.

This is very rich dish, so I accompany it with either a cold, crisp salad of assorted greens or steamed vegetables with a light, herbed, butter sauce.

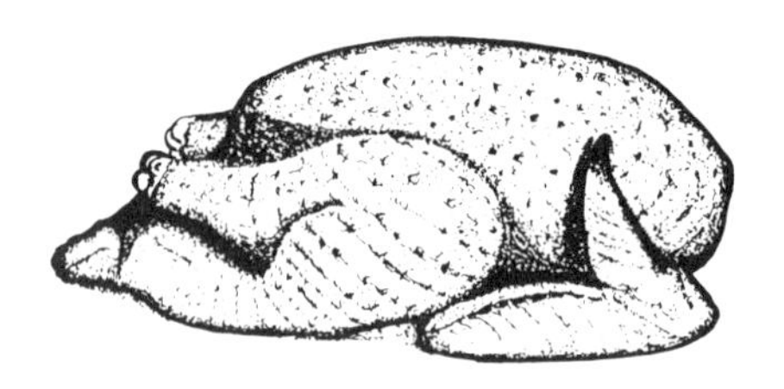

Crepes

½ **Cup water**
½ **Cup milk**
2 **Eggs**
¼ **Teaspoon salt**
1 **Cup flour**
2 **Tablespoons butter, melted**

Put dry ingredients in bowl. Add eggs and blend with a wire whisk until batter is smooth. Add melted butter. Blend. Whisking constantly, pour in milk in a slow, thin stream. Cover with plastic wrap and refrigerate for about 1 hour. If, after making your first crepe, it seems too heavy, beat in a bit of water, a spoonful at a time. A perfect crepe should be about 1/16 inch thick. Lightly oil the skillet. Set over moderately high heat until the pan is just beginning to smoke. Remove from heat and add about ¼ cup of batter into the skillet. Quickly tilt the pan in all directions to spread over the bottom of the pan in a thin film. Return to heat for about 60 seconds. Shake the pan back and forth to loosen the crepe. Flip with either your fingers or a spatula. Brown lightly for about 30 seconds. Remove crepe to a platter. Continue this process until all batter is used.

Chicken Crepes Continued

Chicken Crepes Continued

Crepe Filling

1 Whole chicken
1 Medium onion
3 Tablespoons butter
3 Tablespoons flour
Salt, to taste
Dash of cayenne
1½ Cups chicken stock
½ Cup sherry

Place chicken in a large pot. Cover with cold water. Salt and pepper, to taste. Bring to a boil. Lower heat and simmer for 30-40 minutes, skimming off any foam which comes to the top. Remove chicken. Set aside to cool. Save broth. When chicken is cool, remove chicken from bones and cut into bite-size pieces. Saute onion in 2 tablespoons butter over low heat until limp. Slowly add flour, salt and cayenne pepper, stirring 3-5 minutes. Gradually add chicken stock and sherry. Mixture will thicken. Add pieces of chicken. Simmer 15-20 minutes.

Sauce

2 Tablespoons butter
2 Tablespoons flour
1 Cup milk
1 Cup cheese, shredded (Cheddar, Swiss or Jack)
½ Cup chicken broth
Parsley, freshly chopped

Melt butter in a medium sauce pan over low heat. Add flour, stirring continuously for 3-5 minutes. Slowly stir in the chicken broth and milk. Mixture will begin to thicken. Remove from heat. Stir in ½ cup shredded cheese and blend well. Set aside.

To assemble: Place 2-3 tablespoons chicken mixture in each crepe. Roll and place in a buttered casserole dish. Pour cheese sauce over crepes and sprinkle with additional shredded cheese. Bake 20-25 minutes in a 350° oven. Remove from oven. Top with freshly chopped parsley and serve.

Chicken King Yen

It is interesting to note that the Chinese respect chicken above pork and beef. Live chickens, from a good breed and properly raised, demand several times the price as a frozen or prepackaged one you find in the supermarket. The Cantonese, in particular, go out of their way to preserve the freshness, flavor and tenderness of the chicken. Hundreds of recipes have been created by the Chinese, utilizing all the parts of the chicken and employing many different cooking methods.

Choosing the freshest chicken in the supermarket is difficult; however, try to select a chicken with a yellowish color to its skin, as it will be tastier. Since there are different types of chicken from which to choose, do not let size affect your buying, as size does not guarantee tenderness.

This is the most famous dish from the "King Yen Restaurant." It is served on a bed of thinly shredded cabbage and is sweet, sour, pepper-hot and fragrant all at the same time!

Jim's Featured Pick:

KING YEN RESTAURANT
2984 College Avenue
Berkeley, California
(415) 845-1286

2 Whole chicken breasts, boned
1 Egg
1 Cup flour mixed with 3 tablespoons cornstarch
Oil for deep frying (approximately 2 cups)
¼ Cup vegetable oil
3 Garlic cloves, minced
1 Tablespoon fresh ginger, minced
2 Green onions, chopped
½ Cup chicken broth
2 Tablespoons soy sauce
2 Tablespoons rice vinegar
½ Teaspoon hot chili oil
2½ Tablespoons sugar
⅓ Cup sherry
1 Tablespoon cornstarch (dissolved in 2 tablespoons water)
4 Cups cabbage, thinly shredded
2 Tablespoons sesame seeds

Cut boned chicken breasts (skin left on) into ½'' slices. Whip egg in a small, flat dish. Dip chicken strips in egg. Dredge with flour/cornstarch mixture. Deep fry in oil (375°) for 3-5 minutes or until crisp. Drain on a paper towel. In a wok or heavy sauce pan, heat the ¼ cup of vegetable oil until hot. Add ginger, garlic and green onions, stirring continuously for 10-15 seconds, so as to not let the garlic burn. Add chicken broth, sugar, soy sauce, vinegar, hot chili oil and sherry. Stir additional 10-15 seconds until the mixture is hot and bubbling. Add cornstarch/water mixture. Continue cooking until the sauce thickens, approximately 15-20 seconds. Arrange the cabbage on a serving platter. Place chicken on top of cabbage. Pour hot sauce over chicken. Sprinkle with sesame seeds. Serve at once.

Chicken Napoli

Bryna Laub, soap opera expert, has been a regular on the "People Are Talking" show since 1979. Her weekly commentaries include behind the scene reports about prime time and day time "Soaps." She reveals cast changes, story line previews and actor profiles, as well as trends in the entertainment industry relating to soap operas.

Bryna started a publishing company and produced the first soap opera story line coverage magazine, "Daytime Serial Newsletter." She also lectures extensively on the topic and has written a book titled "The Soap Opera Annual."

When she was my guest in the kitchen we prepared this wonderful chicken casserole that is one of her family's favorites.

4 Tablespoons olive oil
4 Tablespoons butter
1 Red onion, minced
2 Cups whole Italian plum tomatoes, drained
¼ Cup Marsala
2 Garlic cloves, smashed
½ Teaspoon basil, dried
½ Teaspoon oregano
¼ Teaspoon thyme
1 Bay leaf, crushed
¼ Teaspoon whole coriander seed
¼ Teaspoon fennel seed
1 Thick slice orange peel
3 Whole chicken breasts, halved, skinned, boned and flattened
½ Cup flour, seasoned
6 Tablespoons Parmesan cheese, freshly grated
Salt and pepper, to taste
Parsley, freshly minced

Heat 3 tablespoons olive oil and 1 tablespoon butter in a dutch oven. Add onion and saute until golden. Add tomates, Marsala, garlic, basil, oregano, thyme, bay leaf, coriander seed, fennel seed, orange peel, salt and pepper. Simmer for 1 hour. Add parsley after removing from heat. (This sauce is best made two days before using.) Heat 1 tablespoon olive oil and 3 tablespoons butter in a heavy skillet. Add chicken which has been lightly dusted with seasoned flour. Saute until browned, about 3-4 minutes. Place chicken pieces in an ovenproof baking dish and spoon sauce over and around chicken. Sprinkle with Parmesan cheese. Place under preheated broiler for a few minutes until the sauce bubbles. Garnish with a bit of fresh parsley.

Here are two chicken dishes that I prepared during January, my traditional diet month. Both are easily assembled and include several types of fresh vegetables. Each is low in calories, high in nutrition and easy on the budget.

Chicken Stew

1 3 pound chicken, cut up, skin removed
3 Cups cabbage, chopped
1 Cup parsnips, cubed
1 Cup carrots, cubed
1 Cup rutabagas, cubed
1 Cup onions, coarsely chopped
1 Tablespoon garlic, chopped
1 Bay leaf
½ Teaspoon thyme
1½ Cups chicken stock
½ Cup dry white wine
¼ Cup parsley, freshly chopped
½ Teaspoon salt
Freshly ground pepper, to taste

Place the chicken pieces, cabbage, parsnips, carrots, rutabagas, onions, garlic, bay leaf, thyme, chicken stock, wine, salt and pepper into a large pot. Bring to a boil. Cover and simmer for approximately 25 minutes, continuously skimming the fat from the surface. Remove chicken from pot. Pour the broth into a food processor. Puree the vegetables coarsely. Return the chicken and pureed mixture to the pot. Bring to a boil. Simmer for an additional 15-20 minutes. Ladle into individual serving bowls. Top with fresh parsley.

Poached Lemon Chicken

- 2 Quarts chicken stock
- Juice of 1 lemon
- Zest of 1 lemon
- Salt and pepper, to taste
- 1 Sprig fresh thyme (or ¼ teaspoon dried)
- 1 Whole chicken
- 2 Small carrots, finely chopped
- 2 Stalks celery, finely chopped
- 1 Small onion, finely chopped
- 1 Tablespoon cornstarch
- 2 Eggs
- ⅓ Cup lemon juice, freshly squeezed
- Parsley, freshly chopped

Bring chicken stock to a boil. Add juice of 1 lemon and lemon zest. Season with salt and pepper (if using canned chicken stock, do not add additional salt). Add thyme. Place the chicken in pot and reduce heat to a simmer. Cook for 35 minutes, turning once or twice. Remove from heat. Let cool and marinate in broth 1-2 hours. Remove cooled chicken from pot. Cut into pieces and remove the skin. Set aside. Strain the remaining broth and bring to a boil. Reduce the stock, by boiling, to about one half. Add the carrots, celery and onion. Cook until tender, about 20 minutes. Dissolve the cornstarch in a small amount of water (approximately ¼ cup) and add to stock. Stir until thickened. Remove from heat. Whip the eggs and mix with the ⅓ cup of lemon juice. Slowly add to the stock, stirring continuously. Taste for seasonings. Add more lemon juice, if needed. Add chicken pieces to broth. Heat through. Garnish with freshly chopped parsley or fresh mint. Serve immediately.

Chicken with Tomato-Butter Sauce

There are hundreds of spice mixtures in India, each used for different dishes in different ways. "Garam Masala" is the basic spice blend of Northern India. Like curry powder, it varies from region to region depending on the chef. This spice blend is essentially added at the end of the cooking process to lace the dish with the gentle aroma of roasted spices.

"Garam Masala" blend is available in most Indian grocery stores, but sometimes it contains too many spices. To truly enjoy the delicacy of this dish, I urge you to make your own.

Garam Masala

2 Tablespoons cumin seeds
2 Tablespoons coriander seeds
2 Teaspoons cardamon seeds (black or green)
½ Teaspoon whole cloves
2 Bay leaves, crumbled
1 Tablespoon black peppercorns
¼ Teaspoon cayenne pepper

In a heavy fry pan, over medium high heat, combine all the spices and dry roast them, stirring constantly, until they are several shades darker and emit a spicy aroma (about 10 minutes). Let them cool and then grind in a blender or spice mill. This mixture will keep up to three months if stored in an airtight container.

Jim's Featured Pick:

THE PEACOCK
2800 Van Ness Avenue
San Francisco, CA
(415) 928-7001

1 Whole chicken (skin removed)
1 Quart plain yogurt
1 Tablespoon garlic, freshly minced
1 Tablespoon ginger, freshly minced
3 Tablespoons lime juice, freshly squeezed
3 Tablespoons oil
1 Tablespoon Garam Masala
1 Teaspoon salt

Cut up chicken. Place in a bowl or baking dish. Combine remaining ingredients and pour over chicken. Marinate for 12 hours minimum, overnight or up to 24 hours. When ready to prepare, remove chicken from marinade and shake off any excess. Discard marinade. Broil in a preheated oven 10-15 minutes, turning once. Chicken may also be cooked over mesquite or oven roasted. Let cool. Remove meat from bones in large pieces.

Tomato Butter Sauce

3 Tablespoons butter, unsalted
2 Cups tomatoes, pureed
1 Teaspoon Garam Masala
¼ Teaspoon paprika
2 Tablespoons cilantro, freshly chopped
¼ Cup heavy cream

Heat large saute pan over medium high heat. Add butter and pureed tomatoes. Cook 2 minutes until reduced and mixture begins to thicken. Add chicken pieces, Garam Masala, paprika, and cilantro. Cook until chicken is heated through, about 2 minutes. Add heavy cream. Continue cooking about another 2 minutes. Mixture will thicken. Serve garnished with more freshly chopped cilantro. Accompany with steamed rice.

Cornish Game Hens with Apricot Stuffing

When entertaining more than six for dinner, this is the perfect entree; everything can be prepared in advance and popped into the oven at the last minute. I like to prepare this recipe in May and June when fresh apricots are abundant in the market.

This tiny bird is a cross between the domestic rock cornish hen and the Malayan gamecock of India. They usually weigh about 1 pound each, which make them ideal for individual servings. Their flavor combines the subtle sweetness of the grouse and the succulence of the finest young milk-fed chicken.

The game hen can be cooked in almost any way that a chicken can be cooked, roasted, or split and broiled, but I personally think it is best served whole and roasted. This golden brown, apricot glazed game hen has eye appeal that even further enhances its taste appeal!

2 Tablespoons butter
1 Onion, finely chopped
1 Teaspoon sugar
2 Garlic cloves, mashed
½ Cup parsley, freshly chopped
Salt and pepper, to taste
½ Teaspoon rosemary, fresh or dried
½ Teaspoon thyme
2 Cups fresh apricots, chopped
1½ Cups cooked rice
4 Cornish game hens
Additional butter

Heat butter in saute pan. Add onion and sugar and cook until soft. Stir in garlic and parsley. Remove from heat. Add rosemary, thyme, salt and pepper. Cool slightly. In a bowl, combine the onion mixture with the cooked rice and apricots. Set aside. Rinse the hens and pay dry. Loosely pack each with the stuffing. Rub exterior of each bird with softened butter. Bake in a pre-heated 350° oven for approximately 1 hour. Baste every 15-20 minutes with apricot sauce.

Apricot Sauce

1 Can apricot nectar
½ Cup white wine
8 Fresh apricots, quartered
¼ Cup parsley, freshly chopped
2 Green onions, chopped
1 Tablespoon cornstarch (dissolved in 2 tablespoons water)

Combine all ingredients in sauce pan. Cook, uncovered, for 10 minutes or until mixture thickens. Any sauce left over should be passed at the table.

Roast Goose

The goose is a noble bird, famed in history, fable and rhyme. It was written about by Dickens in his infamous "A Christmas Carol" and I'm sure all of us can still remember one or two of the Mother Goose rhymes we learned as children.

People tend to shy away from cooking goose as it has a high fat content. However, with the proper roasting technique, the fat is not a problem. Rendered goose fat is treasured by the chefs of Southern France. It will keep 3-4 months in the refrigerator and freezes perfectly.

Goose has an extraordinary flavor; the breast as well as the legs. The bird bastes itself to a golden brown and underneath the crackling crisp skin is superb dark meat that enhances any holiday feast!

I bake my favorite stuffing (page 107) in a separate casserole and make a savory brown gravy from the pan drippings of the roasted goose.

1 10-12 pound goose
Salt and pepper, to taste
2 Garlic cloves (optional)
1 Onion, quartered
1 Apple, quartered
2 Celery stalks

Remove giblets and neck from body cavity. Cook separately and reserve for gravy or stock. Season inside of cavity with salt, pepper and garlic cloves. Stuff the cavity loosely with the onion, apple and celery stalks. Rub outside with salt and pepper. Prick skin all over to release the fat as it melts. Place the goose on a baking rack, breast side down. Roast in a preheated 350° oven for 1 hour. Turn over. Reduce heat to 325° and continue roasting until tender (total cooking time approximately 3-3½ hours). Pour off the rendered goose fat and strain it through a fine sieve or cheesecloth. Preserve it by placing it in a covered jar in the refrigerator. Goose fat must be clean of all residue or it will spoil. When goose is done, remove from roasting pan onto a heated platter. Garnish with parsley and crab apples.

Roast Pheasant with Brandy Cream Sauce

There are many who will maintain that the duck is the king of all game birds. But to me, for the thickness of the flesh and its exquisite flavor, the pheasant ranks number one.

Upland game birds, such as pheasant, prairie hen, quail and dove live off the fat of the land. Their diet features various seeds, grains, fruits and nuts making them fine eating. The younger the bird, the more tender and succulent. However, you will find that certain recipes using moist heat, as in stewing and casserole dishes with sauces, will turn an old bird into a "spring chicken."

If I'm given some wild birds during the fall season, I will freeze them and save for a small dinner party of 4 to 6 during the holidays. Domestic raised pheasant may be purchased at any local butcher shop, by special request.

As with duck, I prefer to have pheasant roasted; this recipe with the brandy cream sauce is marvelous!

2 Pheasants, approximately 1 pound each
2 Tablespoons butter, softened
4 Strips bacon, cut in half
½ Cup brandy
½ Cup chicken stock
¼ Cup heavy cream

Preheat oven to 375°. Rub the soft butter into the skin of each bird and fill the cavity with your favorite dressing. (You may saute the pheasant livers in a bit of butter and add them to your stuffing.) Do not pack it in too firmly. Secure the openings with string. Truss the birds by tying their legs together. Drape the bacon strips over their legs and breasts and place on a rack set in a shallow baking pan. Sprinkle with salt and pepper. Roast in the oven for about 30 minutes. Remove birds from oven. Heat ¼ cup of the brandy in a small pan. Set alight with a match and pour it flaming over the birds, shaking the pan gently until the flames die out. Baste thoroughly with the accumulated roasting-pan juices. Return pheasants to the oven. Roast for an additional 10-15 minutes or until done. Remove from oven and transfer to a heated platter. Cut and disjoint birds into 4 pieces. Pour the chicken stock and remaining ¼ cup brandy into the roasting pan. Bring to a boil on top of the stove. Boil briskly until sauce begins to thicken, then stir in the cream. Bring to a boil once more. Taste for seasoning. Pour over pheasant and serve immediately.

Orange-Cranberry Turkey Slices

This recipe is from the "Two Week California Turkey Diet" booklet. It is a diet designed by Joan Walsh, the director of California Western Nutritional Service. Besides being low in calories and low in fat, turkey provides a good source of iron, magnesium and vitamins B-6 and B-12.

Turkey slices are readily available at the local market and with a few minutes preparation, this meal can be on the table in less than 30 minutes. A small baked sweet potato and a green vegetable keep the entire meal under 600 calories.

If fresh cranberries are not available, delete the sugar, reduce the orange juice to 2 tablespoons and substitute ¼ cup canned whole cranberry relish for the 1 cup fresh cranberries.

For information about the "Turkey Diet," see Appendix.

1 Pound California turkey breast slices
Salt and pepper, to taste
2 Tablespoons butter, unsalted
2 Tablespoons brown sugar
⅓ Cup orange juice
1 Cup fresh cranberries
¼ Cup raisins
2 Tablespoons green onions, chopped
2 Tablespoons orange-flavored liquer (optional)

Brown seasoned turkey slices in butter 1-2 minutes per side. Remove to a heated platter; keep warm. Add brown sugar, orange juice and cranberries to skillet. Cook 5 minutes or until the cranberries have popped. Stir in raisins, onion and liquer. Heat through. Pour sauce over warm turkey slices.

TRUCK
2
SFFD

VEGETABLES

Corn on the Cob with Flavored Butters
Herbed Green Beans
Potatoes Colcannon
Potatoes Parisienne
Sauteed Carrots with Cucumbers
Stuffed Tomatoes
Risotto with Peppers and Zucchini
Sweet Potatoes with Pecans
Zucchini Pancakes

Corn on the Cob with Flavored Butters

"Corn on the Cob" is an American Tradition that everyone enjoys. Almost anyone who has tasted the different kinds of sweet corn will have his or her favorite. Some insist the white corn is the best and yet others prefer the yellow. Everyone does agree, though, that sweet corn is best eaten at its peak which is as soon as possible after it is picked. There are three basic ways to prepare corn on the cob:

Steaming: Husk and desilk the corn. Steam for 7-8 minutes.

Boiling: Husk and desilk the corn. Plunge into boiling water for 3-5 minutes.

Grilling: Peel back, but do not remove the husks from the ears of corn. Remove the silk. Spread each ear with 1 tablespoon of the flavored butter. Rewrap each ear in its husk and wrap in aluminum foil. Grill the corn 4 inches from the hot coals, turning frequently for about 20 minutes.

Basil Butter

½ Cup butter, softened
1 Cup basil, freshly chopped

Mix butter with basil and blend well. Refrigerate until ready to use.

Curry Butter

½ Cup butter, softened
2 Tablespoons curry powder

Mix butter with curry powder and blend well. Refrigerate until ready to use.

Garlic Butter

½ Cup butter, softened
4 Cloves garlic, peeled and crushed
1 Tablespoon parsley, freshly chopped

Mix butter with garlic and parsley. Blend well. Refrigerate until ready to use.

Herbed Green Beans

The broad term "beans" covers a multitude of culinary delights. There are about 15 different varieties of beans, some of the most common being green beans, string beans, wax beans, lima beans, kidney beans, soy beans and the numerous dried beans.

Herbs give a particularly interesting flavor to vegetables — make them something different. This recipe has an added touch of piquancy — bacon. I serve it often with a variety of entrees.

1 Pound green beans
6 Slices bacon, diced
1 Small onion, sliced
½ Green pepper, chopped
1 Garlic clove, crushed
2 Tablespoons parsley, freshly chopped
1/8 Teaspoon marjoram
1/8 Teaspoon rosemary
1/8 Teaspoon oregano
Pepper, to taste

Trim and wash beans. Cut diagonally into 2 inch pieces. Plunge beans into a small amount of salted, boiling water and cook until tender, 2-4 minutes. Drain. In the meantime, saute the bacon until crisp. Remove with a slotted spoon to a paper towel to drain. To the drippings, add the onion, green pepper, garlic, parsley, herbs and pepper. Saute gently for 5 minutes. Stir the beans and bacon back into the pan just to heat through. Serve at once.

Potatoes Colcannon

Even though I am not Irish, I always prepare a traditional Irish dish on St. Patrick's Day. This recipe is a wonderful combination of textures and flavors... soft, fluffy mashed potatoes, crisply cooked cabbage, sauteed green onions and fresh, aromatic basil. I enjoy it so much I serve it with a meatloaf or a hearty beef roast as well with corned beef!

1 Head cabbage
Water
2 Bunches green onions
1½ Cups milk
½ Teaspoon salt
3 Tablespoons butter, unsalted
2 Pounds potatoes
½ Teaspoon salt
Freshly ground pepper, to taste
¼ Teaspoon dried basil (or ½ teaspoon fresh)
Melted butter

Boil cabbage leaves (enough to make about 2 cups when chopped) in water for about 5 minutes. Drain and chop finely. Set aside. Chop the green onions (utilizing bulbs and tops) and put them to soak in the milk to which the salt and basil have been added. Heat on medium high heat to a boil, adding the butter and simmer slowly until the onions are tender. Boil potatoes, with the skins on, in 1 inch of water until tender, about 30-40 minutes. Test with a fork for doneness. Drain and let cool slightly. Peel and mash with a ricer; this will produce a nice smooth texture. Gradually add the milk mixture and the chopped cabbage leaves. Continue mashing until the leaves are entirely absorbed. Salt and pepper, to taste. To serve, make a depression in the center of each portion and fill the cavity with melted butter. Eat with spoon, from the outside in, dipping a spoonful of the Colcannon potatoes into the butter.

Potatoes Parisienne

This is a simple, elegant accompaniment to almost any main course. The potatoes look lovely with the contrasting color of the fresh parsley and taste marvelous with the delicate sauce of butter, salt and pepper.

3 Whole potatoes, peeled
1 Tablespoon butter
1 Tablespoon oil
Salt and pepper, to taste
Parsley, freshly chopped

Using your melon baller, make as many potato balls as you can. Plunge the balls into boiling water for 3-5 minutes. Drain and place into a skillet with the butter and oil. Salt and pepper, to taste. Saute for 10-12 minutes or until done and they are a nice golden brown. Garnish with freshly chopped parsley. Serves: 3.

Sauteed Carrots with Cucumbers

On a regular basis we have dinner with our dear friends, Weezie and Howard Mott. Weezie is a fabulous chef and Howard is our salmon fishing partner. One evening we were at their home and Weezie prepared sauteed cucumbers as a side dish to our freshly caught salmon... it was marvelous!

2 Cucumbers
6 Medium sized carrots (one per person)
2 Tablespoons butter, unsalted
Salt and pepper, to taste
Parsley, freshly chopped

Peel cucumbers and cut into quarters. Discard seeds and cut into cubes. Steam until crisp/soft, about 3-4 minutes. Rinse under cold water. Set aside. Scrape carrots and cut into diagonal slices. Steam until crisp/soft, about 7 minutes. Rinse under cold water and set aside. When ready to serve, melt butter in skillet. Add cucumbers and carrots and saute for 3-4 minutes, or until heated through. Salt and pepper, to taste. Garnish with freshly chopped parsley.

Stuffed Tomatoes

All tomatoes taste better if vine-ripened. Unfortunately, many of the tomatoes that reach our markets have been picked when green, put into cold storage, and then allowed to ripen in warming rooms. Not surprisingly, a great deal of flavor is lost in this process.

I enjoy tomatoes and in the winter, when they are not at their peak, I like to serve them stuffed, with either a bread crumb and Parmesan cheese mixture or with potatoes as in this recipe. This is another recipe I prepared as part of the "Presidential Dinner" (see index).

4 Tomatoes
4 Boiling potatoes
½ Pint whipping cream
½ Cup Parmesan cheese, freshly grated
½ Cup butter, unsalted
Salt and pepper, to taste
¼ Cup butter, melted

Plunge tomatoes into boiling water 30-45 seconds. Drain and peel. Slice off the top and carefully scoop out the center. Cut a thin slice off the bottom of the tomato so as it will sit flat. Place in a buttered overproof baking dish.

Boil potatoes until tender, about 30-40 minutes. Test for doneness with a fork. Drain and let cool slightly. Peel and mash with a ricer. This will produce a nice smooth texture. Add the whipping cream, Parmesan cheese and ½ cup melted butter. Blend well. Season with salt and pepper.

With a pastry bag fitted with a star tip, pipe the mashed potato mixture into the tomatoes (Up to this point, they may be prepared in advance). Bake in a 350° oven 15 minutes or until heated through. Dribble with melted butter. Place under the broiler until lightly browned on top. Serve at once.

Risotto with Peppers and Zucchini

Our friend, Annette De Nunzio, asked me to be one of six celebrity chefs for the 1986 Risotto Cook-Off and Dinner to benefit the Museo Italo Americano at the Villa Florence Hotel in San Francisco. Each chef was to prepare his risotto recipe for the 250 guests and they would vote for their favorite. Well, the day of the event, I became very ill and was unable to attend, so as a dedicated and supportive wife, Mary went in my place. She enjoyed being the only woman in the "all male" Italian kitchen.

"Risotto" is a uniquely Italian technique for cooking rice. The objective is to cause the rice to absorb, a little at a time, enough hot broth until it swells and forms a creamy union of tender, yet firm grains. Correct heat is very important. It should be hot, but if the liquid evaporates too rapidly, the rice does not cook evenly and it will be soft on the outside and chalky on the inside. If the heat is too slow, the rice becomes gluey, which is even worse. When cooked, the rice should be creamily bound together, neither dry nor runny.

By the way, Mary did not win first place, but rumor has it, she came in a close second!

2 Small zucchini, ¼ inch bite-size pieces
1 Small onion, coarsely chopped
2 Garlic cloves, crushed
1 Cup ham (or prosciutto), cubed
2 Red bell peppers
1 Green bell pepper
4-6 Cups chicken stock
3-4 Tablespoons butter, unsalted
2 Cups Italian rice, (Arborio style)
Parmesan cheese, freshly grated

Saute zucchini, onion, garlic and ham in olive oil over medium heat until soft, about 10-12 minutes. Set aside. Roast peppers under broiler until skins blacken. Place under a damp towel and let rest 20 minutes. When cool, peel skin and discard seeds and white membrane. Cut into ½ inch pieces. Set aside. Heat chicken broth to simmer. In a heavy bottom casserole, heat butter on high. Add rice and zucchini mixture. Stir and coat well with butter. Add ½ cup of the simmering broth, stirring continuously until the broth is absorbed. As the rice dries out, add another ½ cup of the broth, continuing to stir until all the broth is absorbed, using all 6 cups of broth. The rice should be "al dente." Add peppers and mix well. Taste for salt. Turn off heat. Add parmesan cheese and freshly ground pepper. Blend well and serve immediately.

Sweet Potatoes with Pecans

Sweet potatoes are a member of the morning glory family and have been traced back to Hawaii before the year 1250 and to New Zealand a century later. Today, they are grown all over the world, Peru, Spain, China and America.

The sweet potato genus also includes yams, which have a dark orange flesh and are a little sweeter and denser than the sweet potato. Neither store well, so use them while they are fresh.

My sister-in-law, Delores Petersen, is a marvelous cook and is constantly trying and creating new recipes. She prepared this recipe for our Thanksgiving dinner a couple of years ago. It is a great substitute for the traditional candied yams with brown sugar and marshmallows which are served during the holidays.

3 Cups hot mashed sweet potatoes
½ Cup granulated sugar (or ½ cup honey)
½ Teaspoon salt
2 Eggs
¼ Softened butter, unsalted
½ Teaspoon vanilla
½ Cup heavy cream
½ Cup brown sugar
⅓ Cup flour
½ Cup pecans, chopped
3 Tablespoons softened butter, unsalted

In a large bowl, mix sweet potatoes, granulated sugar (or honey), salt, eggs, ¼ cup butter, vanilla and heavy cream. Blend well. Spoon into a buttered baking dish. In a small bowl, combine brown sugar, flour, pecans and 3 tablespoons butter. Blend well. Top sweet potatoes with crumbled mixture. Bake in a preheated 350° oven for 35 minutes.

Zucchini Pancakes

My daughter Jennifer's great grandmother, Ann Fiuren, was born and raised in San Francisco. She was of Irish descent and a survivor of the earthquake of 1906. A wonderful, loving wife, mother, grandmother and great grandmother, she was also a fine cook.

One of her specialties was pot roast with homemade gravy. The dinner also always included steamed carrots, boiled potatoes and zucchini pancakes. The pancakes, hot off the griddle, were covered with dabs of butter and then, if you preferred, a spoonful of hot beef gravy. They are absolutely fabulous!

If you prefer, you may add ½ cup of grated cheese or some freshly chopped basil or parsley.

3 Eggs
2 Tablespoons oil
3 Cups zucchini, grated
1 Small onion, chopped
1 Teaspoon Italian seasoning
Salt and pepper
1 Cup Bisquick (approximately)

Place eggs and oil in a large mixing bowl. Whip, by hand, until well blended. Add zucchini, onion, Italian seasoning, salt and pepper. Blend. Add approximately 1 cup of Bisquick. Mixture should be the consistency of pancake batter. If it is too moist, add a little bit more Bisquick; if it is too dry, add a little bit of milk. Pour batter, about ½ cup for each pancake, onto a hot griddle. Spread to make a circle. Cook until bubbles form and just start to pop on the top surface and edges appear dry. Turn pancake with a wide spatula to lightly brown the other side. Turn pancakes only once. Serve immediately.

DESSERTS

Ann Fraser's Angel Chiffon Dessert

Apple Souffle'

Baked Alaska

Berry Cream Pie

Brazilian Avocado Cream

Brownies

- Jim's Brownies
- Cream Cheese Brownies
- Quick Fudge Brownies
- San Francisco Fudge Foggies

Buckeyes

Butterfinger Chocolate Cream Dessert

Cherry Tart

Chocolate Mousse With Raspberry Sauce

Chocolate Nut Torte

DESSERTS

Coeur A La Creme
Double Fudge Chip Cake
Fresh Fruit Cobbler
Golden Apricot Custard Pie
Italian Thyme and Fig Fruitcake
Mary's Bread Pudding
Mixed Fruit and Nut Cake
Polish Easter Cake
Pumpkin Ice Cream Pie
Pumpkin Pecan Cheesecake
Pumpkin Cake Roll
Rice Pudding
Ricotta Pie
Ross McGowan's Cheesecake
Sweet Potato Pie

Ann Fraser's Angel Chiffon Dessert

When Ann Fraser came to KPIX in 1977, she hosted "The Morning Show." The name of the show was changed to "People Are Talking" when Ross McGowan teamed up with Ann in September, 1978.

Ann began her professional career as an actress, singer, and dancer on Broadway in New York City. She appeared in many musicals and major theatrical productions including "Calamity Jane," "Anything Goes," Noel Coward's "Sail Away," and "Oklahoma." While playing Meg in the New York City Center Production of "Brigadoon" she gave a command performance at the White House for President and Mrs. John F. Kennedy. Ann has also appeared in over two hundred television and radio commercials.

This recipe that we prepared for Father's Day in 1985, is from Ann's mother and has been a family favorite for many years!

6 Egg yolks
¾ Cup sugar
½ Cup lemon juice, freshly squeezed
Rind of 1½ lemons (scored)
1 Tablespoon gelatin, dissolved in ¼ cup water
6 Egg whites
¾ Cup sugar
1 Angel food cake, baked according to directions
1 Pint whipping cream
2 Tablespoons powdered sugar

Put egg yolks, ¾ cup sugar, lemon juice, lemon rind and dissolved gelatin in top of double boiler. Cook until mixture coats a spoon. Cool slightly. Beat egg whites until stiff. Slowly add ¾ cup sugar. Fold gently with egg yolk mixture. Break angel food cake into bite size pieces and add to mixture (using only about one half of the cake). Spoon mixture into a buttered angel food cake pan or spring form pan. Chill for several hours or overnight. To serve, whip cream and gradually add the powdered sugar. Unmold dessert and cover with sweetened whipped cream.

Apple Souffle'

Many people consider the dessert souffle' to be a glorious and exciting finish to a great meal. Puffed up high above its mold in a golden crown, the perfect souffle' comes out of the oven crisp on the outside and creamy in the center. It must be served at once for it falls as it begins to cool. Each serving should include some of the crust as well as a generous scoop from the center.

Although sweet souffle's are lighter and airier than entree souffle's, the basic principles still apply (see Cheese Souffle', p. 264).

I prepared this recipe in January as one of my diet month features. I like to serve it as a dessert or for a special Sunday brunch.

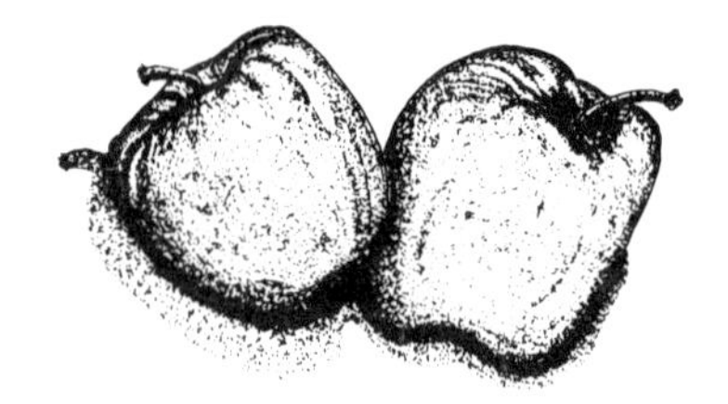

6 Tart apples, peeled, cored and chopped
1 6 ounce can frozen apple juice concentrate (no sugar)
2 Tablespoons sugar
2 Tablespoons cinnamon
8 Egg whites
Powdered sugar
Cinnamon

In a sauce pan, heat apples with apple juice concentrate on high heat. Add sugar and cinnamon. Cook, stirring until the liquid is evaporated and the apples are soft (8-10 minutes). Do not overcook. Transfer to a food processor and puree. Some small pieces of apple may be visible. Transfer to a mixing bowl. Butter the bottom and sides of 6 individual souffle' cups (1 ¼ cup size). Preheat oven to 450°. Whip egg whites until stiff and moist (an option is to beat in ¼ cup sugar at this time, if you feel extravagent). Fold the egg whites into the apple puree. Spoon into the souffle' cups, piling high in the center. Bake 7 minutes at 450°. Reduce heat to 400° for additional 7 minutes. Dust with powdered sugar and a dash of cinnamon. Serve immediately.

Baked Alaska

There are certain festive occasions when you want your dinner to reach its climax with an elaborate dessert, in a blaze of glory, if I may coin a phrase. In such an event, there is nothing that can top a Baked Alaska.

People who have never had it sometimes refuse to believe that ice cream can be baked in the oven and come out firm. But the ice cream is well insulated with sponge cake under it and covered by a meringue.

It is not at all difficult to prepare and it's fun to serve. You can buy the pound cake and ice cream at the supermarket, make a meringue, assemble it, pop it under the broiler, serve and there you are!!

1 Pound cake
¼ Cup brandy
6 Egg whites (save ½ egg shell)
½ Cup powdered sugar
½ Teaspoon cream of tartar
1 Teaspoon vanilla
½ Gallon ice cream
½ Cup chopped nuts
¼ Cup rum or brandy, heated

To prepare the base, place a 1 inch layer of cake on an oven proof dish or even a round board. Dribble with brandy. Prepare the meringue by whipping the egg whites at a high speed. When peaks begin to form, slowly add the powdered sugar, cream of tarter and vanilla. Shape ice cream on top of cake. Working fast, spread the meringue over the ice cream. Garnish with chopped nuts. Insert ½ of an egg shell into meringue. Place under a preheated 500° broiler and brown lightly, 2-3 minutes. Remove from oven. Fill the egg shell with preheated rum or brandy. Set aflame and serve immediately.

Berry Cream Pie

When you think of berries, the first things that come to mind are jams, jellies and pies. I serve this berry pie often as it is easy to prepare, beautiful to present and is always very well received.

3-4 Cups fresh berries, cleaned
½ Cup sugar, more if desired
1 Tablespoon cornstarch
2 Tablespoons water
1 Pint whipping cream**
Dash vanilla extract
3 Tablespoons powdered sugar
1 9" baked pie shell (page 256)

Place berries in a medium bowl. Pour sugar over them. Let stand for 1 hour. Place half the berries and juice in a medium sauce pan. Combine cornstarch and water. Stir into berries. Place over medium high heat and cook for 10 minutes or until thick and clear. Cool. Whip the cream and vanilla extract until stiff. Spread a layer of the cream in the bottom of pie shell. Top with reserved berries. Pour cooled glaze mixture over berries. Spread the remaining cream on top or use a pastry bag fitted with a star tip and decorate top of pie with remaining cream.

**The following combinations may be used rather than 1 pint of whipping cream:

½ whipping cream ½ plain yogurt
½ whipping cream ½ sour cream
½ whipping cream ½ cream cheese

Brazilian Avocado Cream

Mary's friends, Jan and Nile Johnson, live near San Diego, California, and have acres of avocado trees. Every spring they send a couple of boxes of fruit for us to enjoy, so we're continuously looking for new recipes with avocado as the main ingredient. This smooth, tangy avocado cream was originally an experiment, but it is so wonderful, we serve it often.

1 Avocado
Juice of 2 limes
¼ Cup light rum or coconut amaretto
¼ Teaspoon vanilla extract
⅓ Cup plus 2 tablespoons powdered sugar
1 Cup whipping cream
2 Teaspoons finely slivered lime peel

Cut the avocado in half lengthwise; remove the pit. Scoop out the flesh and place it in the food processor. Add the lime juice, light rum or coconut amaretto, vanilla and ⅓ cup sugar. Puree until smooth. Transfer to a large bowl.

In a medium bowl, beat the whipping cream with the 2 tablespoons powdered sugar until stiff. Fold the whipped cream into the avocado mixture. Transfer to individual servings bowls and sprinkle with slivered lime peel. Chill thoroughly before serving. Serves: 4.

Brownies

Brownies are one of America's favorite after school snacks. The best part of making brownies is its simplicity; no special equipment, and even the fanciest take only minutes to prepare. They are, however, quick to disappear minutes after they are out of the oven. Here are four of my favorites, each a bit different!!

Jim's Brownies

2 One ounce squares unsweetened chocolate
¼ Cup butter
1 Cup sugar
2 Eggs
½ Teaspoon vanilla
⅔ Cup flour
½ Cup nuts, coarsely chopped

Grease and flour an 8'' x 8'' square pan.

Melt chocolate and butter, stirring occasionally, until well blended. Remove from heat and let cool to room temperature. Beat eggs, sugar, and vanilla together. Gently fold in the chocolate mixture, flour and nuts, until the white of the flour is lost. Pour into prepared pan. Bake at 300° for 40 minutes. Let cool before cutting.

San Francisco Fudge Foggies

This is the winning recipe from "The Great American Chocolate Cookie" contest at the 1985 San Francisco Fair, where I was a judge. It is sponsored annually by Ghiradelli Chocolate and was won that year by Barbara Feldman of San Francisco.

16 Ounces Ghiradelli sem-sweet chocolate, broken
1 Cup butter, unsalted
⅓ Cup strong black coffee
4 Large eggs
1½ Cups sugar
1½ Teaspoons vanilla
½ Cup flour
2 Cups pecans, coarsely chopped (optional)

In double boiler over low heat, melt chocolate with butter and coffee. Stir until smooth. Remove top of double boiler from heat; set aside. In mixing bowl, beat eggs on high 2-3 minutes until frothy. Gradually add sugar, then vanilla and continue beating until the mixture is very light and fluffy. On low speed, mix the chocolate mixture into the egg mixture just until blended. Add flour, mixing until just moistened. Gently stir in nuts. Pour batter into a buttered 9"x 13" cake pan. Bake at 375° for 30 minutes. Test for doneness with a toothpick. Cool to room temperature before cutting. Yield: 16 large brownies.

Quick Fudge Brownies

½ Cup butter, unsalted
2 Ounces chocolate, unsweetened
1 Cup sugar
2 Eggs
¼ Cup flour
1 Teaspoon vanilla
½ Teaspoon salt
1 Cup walnuts, coarsely chopped

Melt butter and chocolate in heavy saucepan over medium heat. Remove from heat. Add sugar and mix well. Add eggs and stir in quickly. Add flour, vanilla, salt and walnuts. Blend. Pour into a well buttered 8''x 8'' baking dish. Bake at 350° for 40 minutes. Test for doneness. Cool. Cut into one inch squares.

Cream Cheese Brownies

Cream Cheese Filling

2 3 ounce packages cream cheese, at room temperature
¼ Cup granulated sugar
1 Tablespoon flour
1 Large egg
1 Teaspoon vanilla
½ Teaspoon lemon juice

Prepare cream cheese filling by blending all the ingredients together, until smooth, in a food processor or electric mixer. Set aside.

Chocolate Batter

3 Ounces unsweetened chocolate
½ Cup plus 2 tablespoons butter, unsalted
1 Cup plus 2 tablespoons flour
½ Teaspoon baking powder
¼ Teaspoon salt
½ Cup chopped walnuts
3 Large eggs
1¼ Cup granulated sugar
1 Teaspoon vanilla

In a heavy pan, over low heat, melt the chocolate and butter together. Let cool to room temperature. Combine flour, baking powder and salt. Mix well. Add walnuts. In a food processor or electric mixer, beat the eggs until thick and light in color. Gradually beat in sugar and vanilla. Add chocolate mixture and dry ingredients. Blend well. Lightly grease a 9"x 9" pan. Pour in slightly more than half of the chocolate batter. Spoon cream cheese filling evenly over the chocolate. Drop the remaining chocolate batter over the filling, spreading until even. Marbleize by cutting through the batter with a table knife from side to side in a wide zigzag pattern, being careful not to touch the bottom of the dish. Bake in the center of a preheated 325° oven for 40-45 minutes or until a toothpick comes out barely moist. Cool for 6-8 hours before cutting into squares. Yield: 30 brownies.

Buckeyes

"Chocolate and peanut butter" seem to go together like "love and marriage". These rich, crispy cookies are easy to make and easy to enjoy. One recipe makes about 100 which seems like a lot, but once your family has tried them, you'll be making a double batch everytime.

1 Cup butter
2 Cups chunky style peanut butter
1 Pound powdered sugar
3 Cups Rice Krispies
6 Ounces chocolate chips
¼ Stick paraffin

Cream together butter, peanut butter and powdered sugar. Mix in the Rice Krispies. Drop by spoonfuls onto a cookie sheet lined with waxed paper. Chill. When cold, shape into balls by rolling in hands. (Best to keep hands wet). Chill again. Melt chocolate chips and paraffin together over low heat. Dips balls into chocolate. Place on waxed paper and chill until chocolate sets.

Butterfinger Chocolate Cream Dessert

This recipe is from my sister-in-law, Betty Madsen, of Glidden, Iowa. She prepared this for us while we were visiting in the summer of 1986. It is the perfect dessert for a large crowd as it serves 8-10 generously. The recipe should be made in advance and chilled well (preferably overnight) before serving.

2 Cups graham cracker crumbs
1 Cup saltine cracker crumbs
¼ Cup sugar
¾ Cup butter
3 Packages chocolate instant pudding
2 Cups milk
1 Quart vanilla ice cream, softened
1 Pint whipping cream
4 Large Butterfinger candy bars

Melt butter in a saucepan. Blend cracker crumbs and sugar in a mixing bowl. Add butter and mix well. Press crumb mixture into a 9'' x 12'' cake pan. Set aside. Put chocolate instant pudding mix into a food processor. Add milk and beat well. Add softened vanilla ice cream and whip until there are no lumps. Pour into cake pan. Chill for 1 hour or until partially set. Whip cream. Spread over chocolate ice cream mixture. Top with the crushed Butterfingers. Chill several hours or overnight.

Cherry Tart

I served this cherry tart with my Presidential Dinner in February, 1985. It was in honor of George Washington who chopped down his famous cherry tree. Fresh cherries are not available in February, so I used canned cherries and served them atop a rich custard in a tart shell.

Tart Shell

2 Cups flour
½ Cup shortening
¼ Cup butter
½ Cup ice water
1 Teaspoon salt

In a food processor, fit bowl with metal blade. Add the flour, shortening, butter and salt. Process with two or three short bursts, or until the mixture becomes the consistency of coarse meal. Pour the ice water through the feed tube, a little at a time. Stop as soon as the dough begins to form a rough, moist mass. Wrap in plastic wrap and refrigerate 4 hours or longer. Remove ½ hour before using or it will be difficult to work. Roll out dough and press into a 9'' deep dish tart shell or quiche pan. Prick several times with a fork. Cover with foil or wax paper and fill with dried beans, rice or pie weights. Bake in a hot oven (400°) 15 minutes. Reduce heat to 375° and bake an additional 10-15 minutes or until done. Remove pie weights and cool. (A frozen baked pie crust may be substituted).

1 Baked 9 inch deep dish tart shell
2 Cups canned cherries
¼ Cup brandy
1 Cup cherry juice
1 Tablespoon cornstarch
1¼ Cups milk
2 Teaspoons cornstarch
6 Egg yolks
⅓ Cup sugar
1 Teaspoon vanilla
1 Pint whipping cream

Drain cherries well, reserving liquid. Marinate with brandy several hours or overnight.

Mix the milk and 2 teaspoons cornstarch together and bring to a boil. Meanwhile, mix the yolks, sugar and vanilla together with a whisk for one minute. Add the boiling milk mixture and mix well. Place back on the stove and cook, stirring until it thickens. Do not boil. Pour custard into a bowl and chill for a minimum of 3 hours. Whip cream. Blend with custard, folding gently. Fill tart shell. Arrange brandied cherries on top.

Cherry Glaze: Pour cherry juice into a small sauce pan. Add 1 tablespoon cornstarch. Heat until mixture thickens slightly. Spoon over cherries. Chill until ready to serve. This sauce may be prepared in advance.

Chocolate Mousse With Raspberry Sauce Served In Chocolate Shells

Mary and I like to serve this dessert in our home for many reasons... it can be prepared in advance, it has wonderful eye appeal and it is sinfully delicious!!

Chocolate Shells

8 Ounces semisweet chocolate chips (dark or white)
6-8 Scallop shells (any size)

Melt chocolate chips in a heavy saucepan over low heat or in a double boiler. Cool. Wrap outside of scallop shells with aluminum foil. Wrap only about ½ inch underneath; smooth out as many of the wrinkles as possible. With a knife, spread a thin layer of chocolate over the shell. Set in the freezer for about 5 minutes. Spread another layer of chocolate on each shell. Return to the freezer until ready to use (a minimum of 4 hours). Gently remove the foil from the shell and then peel the foil away from the chocolate.

To serve: Place a shell on each dessert plate. With an ice cream scoop, spoon the mousse into the shell. Top with raspberry sauce; and garnish with some fresh raspberries.

Chocolate Mousse

1 Pound semisweet chocolate chips
¼ Pound butter, unsalted
2 Teaspoons instant coffee powder
⅓ Cup water
2 Large egg yolks
⅓ Cup Kahlua liquer
4 Large egg whites (at room temperature)
2 Tablespoons sugar
1 Cup Whipping Cream

Melt chocolate with butter, instant coffee, and water in a heavy saucepan or a double boiler. Mix egg yolks with Kahlua. When chocolate has melted, remove from heat. Add the egg yolks and Kahlua to melted chocolate. Blend. Set aside to cool. Beat the egg whites until stiff. Slowly add the sugar, beating continuously. Spoon on top of the cooled chocolate. Whip the cream until stiff. Gently fold the chocolate/egg white mixture into the whipped cream. Cover and refrigerate at least 4 hours.

Raspberry Sauce

2 Packages frozen raspberries in syrup (thawed)
¼ Cup raspberry jam
1 Tablespoon cornstarch
1 Tablespoon raspberry liquer (optional)
1 Basket fresh raspberries

Place the thawed raspberries in a strainer. Push through to remove the seeds. Discard seeds. Put the strained berries and jam into a small saucepan and bring to a boil. Remove from heat. Add cornstarch to liquer. Stir to dissolve and add to berries. Heat over medium heat, stirring constantly until sauce comes to a boil and begins to thicken. Strain again. Cool. Cover and refrigerate until ready to use.

Chocolate Nut Torte

For all of you chocolate lovers, this torte is heaven; it is dense, rich and decadent. And it's a beauty, all dark and shiny with a chocolate glaze and edged with pecans dipped in chocolate. It will keep well for 4-5 days, but it seldom lasts that long.

Chocolate grows on the cocoa tree or *Theobroma Cacao,* "The Food of the Gods." It is a wide-branching tropical evergreen that grows in many parts of the world, but always within 20 degrees of the equator.

One of the most unusual facts about the cocoa tree is that the blossoms and the fruit do not sprout on the branches, but directly on the main trunk. The fruit, or pods, measure six to fourteen inches in length and two to five inches in diameter. The pods are picked and then broken open. Inside each pod are 25-50 almond shaped seeds. The seeds are placed in baskets or boxes for a period of fermentation to remove the raw, bitter taste and to develop essential oils. Then they are dried and shipped to the manufacturer. Timing, temperature, proportions of various beans and processing are all closely guarded secrets, which is why each companies' chocolate tastes a bit different from another.

4 Ounces semisweet chocolate
¾ Cup pecans
¾ Cup walnuts
½ Cup sugar
¼ Pound butter, unsalted (at room temperature)
3 Eggs, at room temperature
1 Tablespoon rum (light or dark)

Chocolate Glaze

6 Ounces semisweet chocolate, chopped
6 Tablespoons butter, unsalted
Whole pecans or walnut halves

Preheat oven to 375°. Grease cake pan and line with greased waxed paper or parchment. Melt chocolate in double boiler. Cool. Chop nuts with 1 tablespoon sugar in food processor. Set aside. Cream butter and remaining sugar in processor until well blended. Add melted chocolate. Mix until smooth. Add eggs and rum and mix well. Add nuts and blend briefly. Pour into prepared pan. Bake for 25-30 minutes. The cake will be soft, but will firm up as it cools. Remove from oven and cool 20 minutes. Invert onto wire rack. Remove paper and cool completely.

Bake whole pecans or walnut halves in a 350° oven for 10-15 minutes, or until browned. Line a baking sheet with waxed paper. Melt 6 ounces chocolate and 6 tablespoons butter in a heavy saucepan. Dip half of each roasted nut into the glaze and place on the paper lined tray. Cool. Let remainder of glaze cool until slightly thickened. Pour onto middle of cake, tilting the cake so the glaze covers the cake and runs down the sides, using a knife dipped in hot water to smooth the sides. Garnish the top with dipped nuts.

Coeur A La Creme

One of the classic and favorite desserts in France is the "Coeur A La Creme" (Hearts of Cream). It gets its name from the heart-shaped dishes in which it is made and is traditionally served with fresh berries. I prefer to puree some of the berries and spoon the sauce over the dessert and garnish with a few whole berries.

I featured this dessert on the show in the spring, so I used strawberries. The red and white presentation was perfect for Valentine's Day with the "heart-shaped" cream and the strawberry sauce.

Fruit Sauce

10 Ounces fruit (fresh or frozen whole berries)
1 Tablespoon superfine sugar
1 Tablespoon Kirsch liquer

Puree fruit in food processor. Reserve a few whole berries for garnish. Strain through a fine sieve. Stir in sugar and Kirsch. Spoon over prepared Coeur A La Cremes.

8 Ounces cream cheese, at room temperature
1¼ Cups whipping cream
⅓ Cup powdered sugar
1 Teaspoon vanilla

Beat cream cheese with electric mixer or food processor until fluffy. Slowly add ¼ cup of cream and blend. Add the sugar and vanilla. Whip briefly. In a separate bowl, whip the remaining cream until soft peaks are formed. Blend the whipped cream with the cream cheese mixture, folding gently. Line 4 individual or 1 large Coeur A La Creme mold with dampened cheesecloth. It is important to cut the cheesecloth so that it extends well over the edges as you will need the excess. Fill the molds with the cheese mixture. Fold the cheesecloth firmly over the top. Place on a platter and refrigerate a minimum of 8 hours or overnight. To serve, pull back the cheesecloth and invert the molds onto a serving plate. Remove remaining cheesecloth. Top with fruit sauce and whole berries.

Double-Fudge Chip Cake

Laurie Burrows Grad appears weekly as the "Make It Easy" cooking expert on the nationally syndicated "Hour Magazine" show. She came to San Francisco for the gourmet products show in May, 1985. We walked and talked for two days while checking out all the latest cookware, gadgets, and new taste treats. We also exchanged new recipes and ideas for television.

Laurie was my guest chef on the show that week and we prepared her chocolate chip cake (See photo, p. xiii). It is a rich and fudgy dessert, an absolute "must" if you or someone in your family is a chocolate lover! The shortening and eggs for this cake are in the mayonnaise, so don't think they have been forgotten.

I serve this cake without any frosting, but I do especially enjoy it with a scoop of French vanilla ice cream!!

2 Cups all-purpose flour
1⅓ Cups granulated sugar
½ Cup unsweetened cocoa
1½ Teaspoons baking soda
1½ Cups buttermilk
1 Cup mayonnaise
1 Teaspoon vanilla extract
1 12 ounce package semisweet chocolate chips

Preheat oven to 350°. Generously butter 2 large or 5 or 6 mini loaf pans. Lightly dust with flour. Combine flour, sugar, cocoa, and baking soda in a large bowl. Blend. Add buttermilk, mayonnaise and vanilla. Beat until smooth. Stir in chips. Pour batter into prepared pans. Bake for 40-45 minutes for mini loaves; 50-55 minutes for larger loaves.

Fresh Fruit Cobbler

A cobbler, first cousin to the deep dish pie, requires a rich biscuit dough and fresh fruit, baked and served sometimes with a sauce. My favorite way to serve it is with a scoop of rich vanilla ice cream. Although it is generally served as a dessert, I know of some people who serve it at a Sunday brunch or even breakfast.

I always bake it with the fruit that is in season or most abundant at the supermarket. Some of my favorites are peaches, pears, apricots, apples, plums, rhubarb or berries.

The amount of sugar depends on the fruit you are using. For example, if using plums or rhubarb, I'd recommend to use a bit more sugar. However, if using peaches or berries, I'd use a bit less. Also, with peaches or apples, a dash of ground cinnamon would be a nice addition.

½ Cup sugar
1 Tablespoon cornstarch
4 Cups fresh fruit
1 Teaspoon lemon juice
3 Tablespoons shortening
1 Cup flour
1 Tablespoon sugar
1½ Teaspoons baking powder
½ Teaspoon salt
½ Cup milk

Mix sugar and cornstarch in a 2 quart saucepan. Stir in fruit and lemon juice. Cook, stirring constantly until mixture thickens and boils. Boil 1 minute, and continue stirring. Pour into an ungreased 2 quart casserole and keep warm in oven. Cut shortening into flour and blend until mixture is crumbly. Add 1 tablespoon sugar, baking powder and salt. Stir in milk. Drop by spoonfuls onto hot fruit mixture. Bake 25-30 minutes in a preheated 400° oven. Serve warm. Top with heavy cream or ice cream.

Golden Apricot Custard Pie

The fresh apricot season may be short, but thanks to dried apricots their sweet-tangy flavor can be savored all year long. It takes one bite to tell you why California apricots are the aristocrat of the dried fruit world.

Only the best are dried. Fruits for drying must be fully tree-ripened. Because apricots are so delicate, the fruit is all picked by hand. It is a labor intensive process as each tree will be picked several times to ensure fully ripe fruit.

From the fields, fresh apricots are trucked in large bins to drying yards. Here the fruit is washed, pitted and cut, then placed cut side up on large screened drying trays. A light sulphuring process is used to help lock in the nutrients and to protect the apricots' golden color. Then the apricots literally bask in the sun for about three days until dry. Once dried, they are sorted by size, washed and readied for packaging.

It takes six pounds of fresh fruit to make one pound of dried apricots. Only the water is removed, so you are receiving a highly concentrated source of nutritional value several times greater than in fresh or canned fruit.

This recipe was the first place winner in the "dessert" category at the 1984 Apricot Festival. It was submitted by Opal Erickson of Turlock, California.

1 Unbaked 9 inch pie shell (page 256)
¾ Cup dried apricots
½ Cup sugar
4 Eggs
½ Cup apricot nectar
⅓ Cup orange juice, freshly squeezed
⅓ Cup whipping cream
1 Tablespoon lemon juice
½ Pint whipping cream, whipped

In a blender or food processor, finely mince the apricots with the sugar. Add the remainder of the ingredients except the ½ pint of whipping cream. Blend. Pour into the unbaked pie shell. Bake at 450° for 15 minutes. Reduce oven temperature to 350°. Continue baking until the custard is just set in the center, about 20-30 minutes. Cool. Top with whipped cream.

Italian Thyme And Fig Fruitcake

Marion Cunningham was my guest on the "People Are Talking" show in February, 1985. Although born in southern California, she now lives in Walnut Creek, east of San Francisco, where she teaches her own cooking classes. Marion was responsible for the new and complete revision of the 12th edition of "The Fannie Farmer Cookbook" published in 1979.

This recipe for fig fruitcake is from "The Fannie Farmer Baking Book" which Marion also edited. The book encourages even the most timid amateur chef to bake with confidence. It takes the mystery out of baking by offering tips in every category from bread baking, to pies, cakes and cookies. I use her book often and highly recommend that it be part of everyone's cookbook library.

There are several varieties of figs, some round and some oblong and they vary in color from almost white to dark purple. The two most popular dried figs are the Mission and the Calimyrna. The Calimyrna gets its name from a combination of *California* and *Smyrna,* the area in Turkey where it originated. Although Marion recommends the Calimyrna fig in the recipe, any type of dried fig may be substituted.

½ Cup madeira or sherry
½ Cup water
½ Teaspoon dried thyme
1 Cup dried Calimyrna figs, finely chopped
1 ¼ Cups cake flour
¼ Cup yellow cornmeal
1 Teaspoon baking powder
¼ Teaspoon baking soda
½ Teaspoon salt
½ Cup butter, softened
½ Cup granulated sugar
2 Eggs
½ Cup pine nuts
Powdered sugar (optional)

Preheat oven to 350°. Grease and flour a 9 inch round cake pan. Combine the Madeira, water, thyme and figs in a sauce pan. Bring to a simmer and cook for 2 minutes, stirring a few times. Remove from heat and drain, saving ½ cup of the liquid. Set aside. Combine the flour, cornmeal, baking powder, baking soda and salt. Sift together onto a large piece of waxed paper. Cream the butter. Then slowly add the granulated sugar and beat until blended. Add the eggs and beat for a full minute, until fluffy. Add the sifted dry ingredients in two parts alternately with the reserved liquid, beating until smooth after each addition. Stir in the figs and pine nuts. Spread evenly in the prepared pan and bake for about 45-55 minutes or until a toothpick inserted in the center of the cake comes out clean. Let rest in the pan 5 minutes, then turn out onto a rack to cool completely. If you wish, dust the top with powdered sugar before serving. Slice very thin.

Mary's Bread Pudding

Bread pudding is one of those traditional dishes that is the homiest and heartiest of desserts.

When Mary was in the 4-H Club many years ago, she was given this recipe by a friend's grandmother. It is different from the traditional bread pudding (stale bread, milk, eggs, cinnamon and sugar) as it includes apples, pecans, cream cheese and is topped with a cinnamon-pecan meringue.

I like to serve it warm with a bit of whipped cream or a small scoop of rich vanilla ice cream.

1 Cup brown sugar, firmly packed
¾ Cup water
2 Tablespoons rum (optional)
3 Whole cloves
1 Cinnamon stick
9 ½ inch thick slices stale bread, crusts removed
¾ Cup butter
4 Ounces cream cheese, softened
1 Cup pecans, chopped
1 Large pippin apple, peeled and chopped
½ Cup raisins
2 Egg whites
3 Tablespoons brown sugar
1½ Teaspoons cinnamon
Whipped cream or French vanilla ice cream

Combine ⅔ cup pecans, chopped apple and raisins in a small bowl. Set aside. In a medium saucepan, add 1 cup brown sugar, water, rum, cloves and cinnamon stick. Bring to a boil, stirring constantly. When it comes to a boil, let boil for one minute. Strain and set aside. Melt approximately 4-5 tablespoons of butter in a saute pan. Add bread slices to lightly color on each side. Add more butter for each group of bread slices. When all the bread is browned, melt remaining butter. Set aside. Butter a casserole dish (3-4 inches high). Place bread on bottom of casserole. Cover with ⅓ of pecan, apple, raisin mixture. Pour ⅓ of the strained sauce over top. Top with ⅓ of the cream cheese (in dabs). Repeat this process three times. Pour remaining butter on top. Press down gently on bread slices. (Up to this point may be done in advance.) Approximately 1 hour before you plan to serve, beat egg whites until stiff. Gently fold in ⅓ cup pecans, 3 tablespoons brown sugar and cinnamon. Spread over bread pudding. Bake in a preheated 350° oven for 35 minutes. Turn oven off and let pudding stand until you are ready to serve.

Mixed Fruit And Nut Cake

This mixed fruit and nut cake recipe comes from a friend, Susan Costner. Susan published a book, "Gifts of Food" in which she compiled more than 150 delectable recipes for edible gifts. Together with complete directions for packaging, she also has a section that tells how to label, tie, bag, box, paint and decorate an endless assortment of containers.

This particular fruit cake, wrapped in a bright colored cloth with sprigs of holly or a Christmas ornament on top, makes a wonderful gift during the holidays.

10 Ounces figlets (small dried figs)
12 Ounces pitted prunes
10 Ounces pitted dates
10 Ounces muscat raisins
½ Cup cognac
1½ Pounds salted mixed nuts
6 Ounces whole pecans
1½ Cups flour
1 Cup sugar
1 Teaspoon baking powder
6 Eggs, beaten

In a very large bowl, combine the fruits and cognac. Let stand for 15-20 minutes, until the liquid is absorbed. Line 2 pans (8½" x 4½" x 2½") with aluminum foil, pressing out all the wrinkles, allowing 1 inch of foil to overlap the edges of the pan all the way around. Reserve 1½ cups of the mixed nuts and set aside. Add remaining nuts to the fruit mixture. Add the flour, sugar, and baking powder to the fruit and nut mixture. Stir until well combined. Pour the eggs over the mixture and mix well. Divide the batter into 2 equal parts and pack in the foil-lined pans, firmly, to eliminate air pockets. Sprinkle the reserved nuts on top, pressing them firmly into the batter. Bake in a preheated 300° oven for 1½ hours, until a knife inserted into the center comes out clean. Cool the cakes in their pans for 30 minutes. Use the overlapping edges of foil to lift the cakes from their pans. Carefully peel off the foil. Cool the cakes completely on a cake rack before wrapping tightly in foil. Refrigerated, the cakes keep for 1 month.

Pumpkin Ice Cream Pie

Laurie Burrows Grad appears as the "Make It Easy" cooking expert for "Hour Magazine". She is also the food editor for the "Los Angeles Magazine" and a contributing columnist for several other food publications.

Laurie was a guest chef on the "People Are Talking" show in October, just in time to show us how to prepare this fabulous Pumpkin Ice Cream Pie for the fall holidays!

If you wish to use fresh pumpkin, see Volume I, Page 214, for instructions.

Gingersnap Crust

25 Gingersnaps, crushed (1½ cups)
5 Tablespoons unsalted butter, softened
1/3 Cup granulated sugar

Crush gingersnaps. Reserve 2-3 tablespoons for topping. Mix crumbs with butter and sugar in a bowl. Press into a 9 inch pie plate. Chill.

Pumpkin Filling

1½ Cups canned (or fresh) pumpkin
½ Cup granulated sugar
½ Teaspoon cinnamon
¼ Teaspoon ground nutmeg
¼ Teaspoon salt
1/8 Teaspoon ground ginger
1/8 Teaspoon ground allspice
1 Quart vanilla ice cream, softened
½ Cup pecans, chopped

In a large bowl, combine pumpkin, sugar, cinnamon, nutmeg, salt, ginger and allspice. Mix well. Fold pumpkin mixture into softened ice cream. Stir in pecans and spoon into pie shell. Sprinkle with reserved gingersnap crumbs. Freeze, uncovered, for 30 minutes, or until set. Cover with plastic wrap or foil. Keep frozen until ready to serve. Remove from freezer 10 minutes before serving. Cut into wedges and serve icy cold.

Polish Easter Cake (Babka)

The crowning glory to a festive Polish dinner is the pastry. A national specialty is an Easter cake called "Babka Wielkanocna". Babka in Polish translates to "Grandmother", although it sounds as if it should translate to "Baby". It is a delectable yeast cake made of rich dough containing many egg yolks, a lot of butter and is flavored with white raisins, grated lemon and orange rind.

In years past when yeast was homemade and unpredictable, Polish women placed their dough on a feather pillow to rise. Everyone was expected to tiptoe about and whisper. Fortunately, today we have packaged active dry yeast that is almost fool proof as well as electric mixers and controlled ovens.

Traditionally it is baked in a two quart "Gugelhopf" pan or a "Turk's Head" mold. Both molds are available at a gourmet specialty store. A bundt cake pan is a perfect substitute and much less expensive.

Although the Polish like to feature this cake on Easter Sunday, I have found that it is also a perfect weekend brunch treat when feeding a crowd.

Icing

2 Cups powdered sugar
¼ Cup cold water
2 Teaspoons fresh lemon juice

Put all ingredients in a mixing bowl. Blend well. Pour the icing slowly over the top of the warm cake, allowing it to run down the sides.

1¼ Cup lukewarm milk (110°-115°)
1 Package active dry yeast
6 Tablespoons sugar
3-4 Cups all purpose flour
½ Teaspoon salt
10 Egg yolks (at room temperature)
¾ Pound plus 2 tablespoons unsalted butter, softened
1 Cup white seedless raisins
2 Tablespoons finely grated orange peel
1 Tablespoon finely grated lemon peel

Warm milk in saucepan. Remove from heat and let cool to lukewarm. Add sugar, yeast and salt. Let the mixture stand for 2-3 minutes, then stir to dissolve the yeast completely. Set aside for approximately 10 minutes in a warm, draft-free place. Place 3½ cups flour in a mixing bowl. Add yeast mixture and egg yolks. Beat hard. Add butter, a few tablespoons at a time. Mix well. The dough should be firm enough to be gathered into a medium-soft ball. If necessary, stir in up to ¼ cup more flour, a tablespoon at a time. Transfer the dough to an electric mixer equipped with a kneading hook and knead for about 20 minutes or until the dough is very smooth, glossy and elastic or knead by hand for about 40 minutes. Shape the dough into a ball. Place it in a lightly buttered bowl and dust the top with flour. Drape a towel over bowl and set aside in a warm, draft-free place for about 60 minutes. Punch the dough down with a single blow of your fist and into it knead the raisins, orange peel and lemon peel. Blend gently and BRIEFLY. Place in a well buttered and floured mold. Drape with a towel and again place in a warm, draft-free place for an additional hour (or until doubled in volume). Bake in a preheated 375° oven for 40 minutes or until golden brown. Turn the cake out onto a wire rack and let it cool briefly at room temperature before icing.

Pumpkin Pecan Cheesecake

Cheesecakes are the most sensuous of desserts. Others may please, even delight the palate, but there is something special about cheesecake...something almost sinful in the richness...something that hints at the possibility of pleasure without limit.

The most essential ingredient in any cheesecake is, you guessed it, cheese. The cheeses most commonly used are cream cheese, cottage cheese and ricotta. Many recipes also call for cream, either sweet or sour. Usually the cream is added to lighten the cake or to provide a richer flavor. Every dessert cheesecake requires a sweetening of some kind. Most use granulated sugar; however, it is possible to use brown sugar or honey in almost all recipes.

Even people who do not like pumpkin pie enjoy this creamy cheesecake with its nutty crust, subtly spiced filling and praline topping.

Crust

½ Cup pecans, finely chopped
1 Cup graham cracker crumbs
⅓ Cup light brown sugar, firmly packed
5 Tablespoons butter, melted

To make the crust, combine the pecans, graham cracker crumbs, brown sugar and butter in a mixing bowl and blend well. Press this dough into a 9 inch springform pan on the bottom and sides in an even layer. Chill for 30 minutes.

Filling

3 **Cups (3 8-ounce packages) cream cheese, softened**
¾ **Cup light brown sugar, firmly packed**
¾ **Cup granulated sugar**
5 **Eggs**
3 **Tablespoons flour**
1 **Teaspoon cinnamon**
½ **Teaspoon ground cloves**
½ **Teaspoon ground ginger**
¼ **Teaspoon grated nutmeg**
2 **Cups pumpkin puree**
2 **Tablespoons praline or amaretto liqueur**
¼ **Cup heavy cream**
½ **Cup pecans, finely chopped**

Topping

½ **Pint whipping cream**
½ **Cup pecans, finely chopped**

To make the filling, cream together the cream cheese and sugars in the food processor. Then beat in the eggs, one at a time. In a separate bowl, stir the flour and spices together. Beat this into the cream cheese mixture. Add the pumpkin, liqueur and cream. Blend. Stir in the pecans. Pour the filling into the crust. Bake for 1 hour and 45 minutes in a preheated 325° oven, or until the top is golden brown. Cool in the pan, on a wire rack. Cover and refrigerate for at least 3 hours. To serve, remove the sides from the pan and place the cake on a serving dish. Top with whipped cream and pecans.

Pumpkin Cake Roll

Every fall they hold a pumpkin festival near Half Moon Bay, a small community along the coast south of San Francisco. There are fields of pumpkins everywhere. It is a beautiful sight...the blue Pacific on one side and the bright orange pumpkins on the other!

Pumpkins have been growing in the Americas for thousands of years. They were a staple Indian food and were widely used by the New England colonists as well. We serve pumpkin pie at Thanksgiving to remember the pilgrim's first harvest feast.

Don't wait until Thanksgiving to serve this light, creamy pumpkin cake; it's to be appreciated the year around.

Cream Cheese Mixture

1 Cup powdered sugar
4 Ounces cream cheese
4 Tablespoons butter
½ Teaspoon vanilla

In food processor or mixer, combine all ingredients. Process until smooth.

3 Eggs
1 Cup sugar
2/3 Cup pumpkin
1 Teaspoon lemon juice
3/4 Cup flour
1 Teaspoon baking powder
2 Teaspoons cinnamon
2 Teaspoons ginger
1/2 Teaspoon nutmeg
1/2 Teaspoon salt
1 Cup pecans, chopped
Powdered sugar

Preheat oven to 400°. Line the bottom of a jelly roll pan (15'' x 10'' x 1'') with waxed paper or foil, trimmed to fit. Butter the paper. Sift flour, baking powder, salt, ginger, cinnamon, and nutmeg together. Beat the eggs until light and foamy. Continue beating, adding the sugar slowly, until mixture is very thick and at least doubled in bulk. Sprinkle the sifted dry ingredients over the batter and fold them in gently. Fold in the pumpkin and lemon juice. Pour into prepared pan. Bake for 12-15 minutes or until the cake is delicately browned and the top springs back when lightly touched. Loosen the cake around the edges and turn it out on a cloth. Sprinkle evenly with powdered sugar. Working quickly while the cake is warm, carefully remove the paper. Cut off the crip edges of the cake. Starting with the long side, gently roll up the cake right along with the towel. (The towel keeps the cake from sticking to itself.) Place the roll, towel and all, on a cake rack to cool. When cool, unroll the cake and remove the towel.

To assemble: Gently spread cream cheese mixture over the cake. Sprinkle with the pecans. Reroll the cake and dust the outside with powdered sugar.

Rice Pudding

My brother, Bob and I were members of a duck club in the Sacramento Valley for about five years. The owner of the club had a small house in the town of Maxwell, so we'd go up on Friday night, eat dinner at the local restaurant, stay overnight and get up early and hunt the next day. The Sacramento Valley is abundant with rice fields which are perfect for good duck hunting.

The only restaurant in the town of Maxwell is the "Chateau Basque". The owner, Pierre, tends the bar and his wife, Olga, tends the kitchen. She serves traditional family style meals of tremendous portions and always makes sure you leave fully satisfied.

Olga always includes a boiled rice dish on her menu and would utilize any leftovers in making this tasty rice pudding. The orange peel gives it a very unique, wonderful flavor. For a more custardy pudding, two eggs may be added in the cooking process. Also, if you prefer, you may add raisins, although Olga thinks it's better without.

3 Cups cooked rice
2½ Cups milk (or half milk and half cream)
1 Cup sugar
Dash of salt
1 Teaspoon vanilla
Peel of an orange
Dash of mace (or cinnamon)

Combine rice, milk, sugar, vanilla and orange peel in a sauce pan. Cover and cook on low heat until all the liquid is absorbed. Discard orange peel. Serve hot or cold with some heavy cream. Top each serving with a dash of mace or cinnamon.

Ricotta Pie

This is a recipe from the J.C. Penney, ''Salute To Italy'' celebrity cookbook that I featured on the show. A percentage of all proceeds from the sales of this book go to various special charities.

The celebrity I chose was Sophia Loren. Sophia is a very beautiful Italian actress who has played in many great movies. One of her first was ''Quo Vadis'' where she was an ''extra''. I believe her only academy award was for her performance in ''Two Women'', a fabulous movie.

One of the key secrets of any successful pie is its crust. The recipe tells how to make the crust by hand, however, I used the food processor and obtained the same result. I recommend the dough ball be chilled at least 2 hours or more before using.

Sophia was unable to be my guest on the show, but I went ahead and prepared her recipe of ricotta pie, this light cheesecake dessert....Delicious cheesecake from a delicious cheesecake!!

1 Cup flour
½ Cup sugar
Pinch of salt
¼ Teaspoon grated lemon rind
½ Cup butter
1 Egg yolk, beaten
Water, as needed
1 Pound ricotta cheese
1 Cup sugar
1 Egg
½ Teaspoon lemon rind
2 Egg yolks
2 Tablespoons golden raisins
2 Tablespoons pine nuts
Diced orange and citron peel (optional)
Powdered sugar

Sift together flour, ½ cup sugar and salt in a bowl. Add ¼ teaspoon lemon rind. With a pastry blender, work butter into the flour until it resembles coarse crumbs. Blend in 1 egg yolk. Add water by droplets until pastry can be worked into a ball. Cover with plastic wrap and refrigerate for at least one hour. Roll out pastry and fit into a 9'' pie pan. Flute edges. Set aside. Beat ricotta with ½ cup sugar and the egg until smooth. Add the ½ teaspoon lemon rind, ½ cup sugar and 2 egg yolks, beating until well blended. Add the raisins, nuts and candied fruit. Pour into the prepared pie shell. Bake in a preheated 350° oven for approximately 30 minutes. If pie is browning too quickly, cover lightly with aluminum foil. Serve cold, dusted with powdered sugar.

Ross McGowan's Cheesecake

Ross McGowan has been the co-host of the award winning "People Are Talking" show with Ann Fraser since September, 1978.

He was born in Los Angeles and raised in San Jose, California. While going to San Jose State, he worked for a local radio station. Many of our viewers remember Ross as a top 40 disc jockey for KYOS Radio in Merced, California, where he worked after graduation. Prior to joining the "People Are Talking" show, he hosted a live talk and entertainment show in Seattle, Washington.

Ross is quite a cheesecake expert, eating, as well as cooking. This recipe is his own creation. We prepared it for Mother's Day, 1985 and the mail response was tremendous!!

1 ¼ Cups plain graham cracker crumbs
¼ Cup melted butter
1 8 ounce package cream cheese
½ Cup sugar
1 Tablespoon lemon juice
½ Teaspoon vanilla
Dash salt
2 Eggs
1 Cup sour cream
2 Tablespoons sugar
¼ Teaspoon vanilla

Combine crumbs and butter. Press into an 8 inch pie pan or a springform pan. Set aside. In a mixer or food processor, beat cream cheese until fluffy. Gradually pour in the sugar. Add the lemon juice, vanilla and salt. Blend. Add the eggs one at a time, beating each well, until blended. Pour the filling into the crust. Bake in a preheated 325° oven for 25-30 minutes or until set. Check by inserting a toothpick into the center; it should come out clean. When completely baked, combine sour cream, sugar and vanilla. Spoon over top. Bake for an additional 10 minutes. Chill well before serving.

Sweet Potato Pie

On the "People Are Talking" staff, the associate producer who helps me co-ordinate my cooking segments is Karen Stevenson. Once a month, we will sit down and discuss, plan, and organize my weekly segments for 4-6 weeks in advance.

When I suggested preparing a sweet potato pie, Karen insisted that I use this recipe from her friend, Richard, who lives in New Jersey. She said it was the best; Karen was right. I can always tell when a recipe is a hit with our viewers by the mail response; we received over 2,000 requests, within five days, for this popular dessert.

2 Cups flour
½ Cup shortening
¼ Cup butter, unsalted
½ Cup ice water
1 Teaspoon salt
4 Cups cooked sweet potatoes (or yams)
1 Cup sugar (or ¾ cup honey)
3 Eggs
½ Cup butter, unsalted
1½ Teaspoons cinnamon
1 Tablespoon vanilla
1 Tablespoon lemon juice
½ Cup heavy cream

PIE CRUST: In a food processor, fit bowl with metal blade. Add the flour, salt, shortening and ¼ cup butter. Process with two or three short bursts, or until the mixture becomes the consistency of coarse meal. Pour the ice water through the feed tube, a little at a time. Stop as soon as the dough begins to form a rough, moist mass. Wrap the dough in plastic wrap and refrigerate 4 hours or longer. Remove the dough ½ hour before using or it will be difficult to work with. Roll out dough and fit into a 9'' or 10'' pie plate, or a deep dish tart pan.

FILLING: Puree the sweet potatoes in the food processor until smooth. Add ½ cup butter, sugar, eggs, cinnamon, vanilla, lemon juice and heavy cream. Blend well. Pour into the unbaked pie shell. Bake in a preheated 350° oven for approximately 50 minutes or until a knife inserted comes out clean.

TRUCK
2
SFFD

POTPOURRI

California Rice
Chili Rellenos
Calzone
Cheese Souffle'
Chocolate Christmas Trees
Egg Nog
Golden Holiday Punch
Country Picnic Loaf
Kiwi Freezer Jam
Sweet Pepper Relish
Peanut Brittle
Nut Crunch
Seafood Dirty Rice
Upside Down Garlic Bomb
Yogurt Berry Pancakes

California Rice

This is a recipe Mary brought with her from San Diego where she lived before moving to the Bay Area. It is a perfect accompaniment to a variety of entrees: fried chicken, bar-b-qued spare ribs, chili rellenos or even grilled pork chops. It is a rich, creamy blending of several distinctive flavors, onions sauteed in butter, sharp cheddar cheese, tangy sour cream and the spice of oregano and green chilies.

½ Cup butter, unsalted
1 Cup onion, chopped
4 Cups cooked rice
1 Cup cottage cheese
2 Cups sour cream
2 Cups cheddar cheese, grated
1 7 ounce can diced chilies
2 Tablespoons parsley, freshly chopped
1 Teaspoon dried oregano
Freshly ground pepper, to taste

Lightly brown onions in butter. Remove from heat and pour into a large mixing bowl. Add cooked rice, cottage cheese, sour cream, parsley and oregano. Mix gently. In a buttered casserole (3-4 inches high) layer ⅓ of the rice mixture. Top with ⅓ of the diced chilies and ⅓ of the grated cheddar cheese. Follow same procedure a total of three times, topping with balance of cheddar cheese. Bake at 350° for approximately 35-40 minutes or until casserole bubbles. Serves: 8.

Chili Rellenos

There is always an exclamation of pleasure when a platter of golden, puffy chili rellenos are presented at the table. Chili rellenos are prepared with the large poblano chilies, stuffed with cheese, coated with a light batter and fried. You bite through the slightly crisp, mild chili to experience the creamy smooth melted cheese... it's fabulous!

6 Poblanos chilies (or substitute canned whole chilies)
3 Eggs, separated
1 Small onion, finely chopped
2 Tablespoons flour
Salt and pepper, to taste
Dash cumin powder
Mozzarella, Jack or Cheddar cheese
Oil for deep frying

If using fresh chilies, put under the broiler and let skin blister and burn. When blistered, wrap in a damp towel for about 20 minutes. Peel, the skin will then flake off easily. Slit sides and remove the seeds. Stuff with small wedges of cheese. Set aside while preparing the batter. Beat the egg whites until stiff. In a separate bowl, beat yolks until creamy and add the onion, cumin, salt, pepper and flour. Heat oil to 375° or until it starts to smoke. Gently fold the egg whites with the egg yolk mixture. Place a spoonful of batter (enough to hold a chili) in the pan. Place a chili on top and cover with more batter. Fry, turning only once, until golden brown. Drain on paper towels. Serve warm with sour cream and salsa.

Calzone

I was in San Jose, California, one day and was invited to eat lunch at the "Stuft Pizza" Restaurant. They prepare wonderful pizzas, but their "Calzones" are the house speciality. A calzone is simply a pizza folded in half like a turnover.

I have prepared homemade pizzas on the show, so I decided to use the same dough recipe and make calzones. They are fun to prepare and you can use any combination of fillings you prefer. Let everyone in the family create their own... ..."personalized" stuffed pizzas at home.

Suggested Fillings

Meats:
- Italian Sausage
- Hamburger
- Pepperoni
- Salami
- Canadian Bacon
- Ham

Cheeses:
- Mozzarella
- Monterey Jack
- Cheddar
- Swiss
- Parmesan

Fish:
- Anchovies
- Shrimp
- Smoked Oysters
- Tuna

Vegetables:
- Onions
- Peppers
- Zucchini
- Asparagus
- Garlic
- Tomatoes
- Mushrooms
- Olives

Pizza Tomato Sauce

2 Tablespoons olive oil
1 Onion, chopped
1 Garlic clove
1 10 ounce can Italian pear shaped tomatoes
½ Cup red wine
1 Tablespoon oregano
1 Teaspoon Italian seasoning
1 Teaspoon basil
Salt and pepper, to taste

Heat oil over medium heat. Add onion and garlic. Saute gently 3-4 minutes. Add remaining ingredients and simmer approximately 30 minutes. Puree sauce in blender or food processor. Pass thru a sieve, pressing with a wooden spoon. Yield: about 2 cups.

Pizza Dough

1 Envelope dry yeast
½ Cup warm water (110°-115°)
4 Cups flour
1 Cup warm milk
2 Tablespoons olive oil
1 Teaspoon salt

Dissolve yeast in warm water. Let stand for 10 minutes. Put flour, milk, olive oil and salt in food processor and combine until smooth, about 30 seconds. Turn onto a floured work surface and hand knead until smooth and elastic. Place in a greased bowl and cover with a towel. Let rise until doubled in size, about 1½ to 2 hours. Divide dough into four pieces and roll out to round shapes, ¼ inch thick and 12 inches in diameter. Brush with olive oil. Top with tomato sauce and your favorite fillings. Pile high with cheese and add a little more sauce. Fold in half and pinch edges to seal. Cut a hole for steam to escape. Brush with oil. Bake in a preheated 450° oven for 20-25 minutes.

Cheese Souffle'

Souffle's, French for "breath", have a built-in limit for holding their puff. The understanding in most kitchens is "A souffle' does not wait for you, you wait for the souffle'."

Mastering the art of making a good souffle' is only a matter of learning a few essential techniques. The glory and lightness of a souffle' is largely a matter of how voluminously stiff the egg whites have been beaten. They should mount seven or eight times their original volume. Room temperature egg whites are best. When folding the egg whites into the flavored sauce, they should be incorporated very gently and delicately so that they will retain as much of the volume as possible.

When serving any souffle', puncture the top lightly with a serving spoon and fork and spread apart. Each serving should include some of the crust and some of the filling.

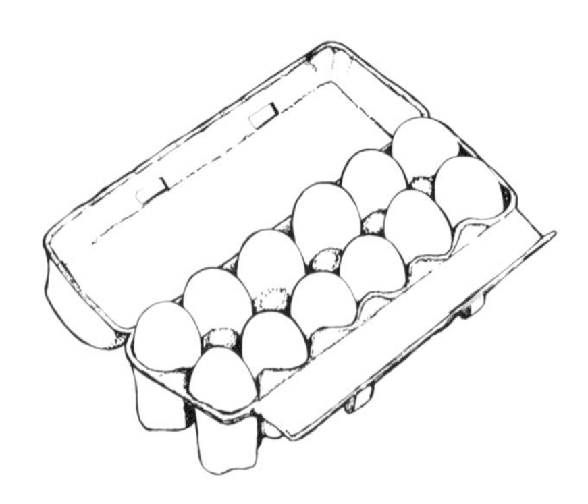

1 Tablespoon butter, softened
1 Tablespoon Swiss cheese, freshly grated
3 Tablespoons butter
3 Tablespoons flour
1 Cup hot milk
½ Teaspoon salt
Pinch of white pepper
4 Egg yolks
6 Egg whites
1 Cup cheese, freshly grated

Preheat oven to 400°. Grease the bottom and sides of a 2 quart souffle' dish with soft butter. Add the 1 tablespoon of Swiss cheese, tipping the dish to coat the bottom and sides. Set aside. In a sauce pan, melt 3 tablespoons of butter. Stir in the flour with a wooden spoon and make a roux. Do not brown. Remove from heat and stir in the hot milk. Beat with a whisk until well blended. Season with salt and pepper. Return to heat and cook until smooth and thick. Remove from heat and beat in the egg yolks one at a time, alternating with the cup of grated cheese. In a large bowl, beat the egg whites until they form stiff peaks. A pinch of salt and some cream of tartar may be added at this time. Stir a large spoonful of the egg whites into the egg yolk sauce to lighten it. Lightly fold in the remaining egg whites. Gently pour the souffle' mixture into the prepared dish. If you use a shallow mold, tie a well-buttered paper collar around the dish to hold the souffle' as it rises. Place the souffle' on the middle shelf of the oven and immediately turn the oven down to 375°. Bake for 25-30 minutes or until the souffle' puffs up about 2 inches above the rim of the dish and is lightly browned. Serve at once.

Chocolate Christmas Trees

Our friend, Sue Kirkham, is from Australia and is a terrific cook. We are always exchanging recipes and creating new ones when we get together.

Sue gave me this idea one Christmas to use on the show. It is an absolute "must" for you to prepare with your children. It is fun, easy to do and like real Christmas trees, every chocolate tree is special and unique. It is also perfect to serve at a holiday buffet as guests may help themselves by breaking off a "limb" at a time.

1 Pound chocolate (milk or semi-sweet)
¼ Cup grated coconut
¼ Cup chopped nuts
Powdered sugar

Melt chocolate over low heat in a heavy saucepan or double boiler. Reserve ¼ cup. Remove melted chocolate from heat. Let cool 10 minutes. Stir in coconut and nuts. On a cookie sheet lined with waxed paper, make crosses of chocolate. Make in various sizes starting from about 6 inches down to 2 inches. Chill well. Melt remaining ¼ cup chocolate. Stack crosses of chocolate, starting with the largest first. Use melted chocolate in between crosses to bind together. Dust lightly with powdered sugar. Chill until ready to serve.

Egg Nog

To some traditionalists, including myself, Christmas would not be the same, in fact would be rather bleak, without a huge punch bowl of egg nog. If you prefer, you may substitute rum extract for the rum or brandy.

12 Egg yolks
¾ Cup sugar
3 Cups heavy cream
2 Cups rum or brandy
¼ Teaspoon salt
12 Egg whites
Freshly grated nutmeg

Beat egg yolks until lightly mixed. Slowly beat in sugar and cream. Add rum or brandy. Whip egg whites separately. Fold into yolk mixture. Top with nutmeg. Serves: 12.

Golden Holiday Punch

Often during the holidays, we entertain a large group of friends and their families. We like to provide a cold punch (Volume I, p. 224-225), a warm punch, egg nog and wine or champagne. This warm, spicy punch is one of our favorites.

1 Tablespoon whole allspice
10 Whole cloves
2 Cinnamon sticks
3 Cups apple cider
1 12 ounce can carrot juice
½ Lemon, freshly squeezed

Place all ingredients in a sauce pan. Simmer for 20-30 minutes. Remove cloves and cinnamon sticks. Serve immediately. Yield: 4 cups.

Country Picnic Loaf

A planned picnic can happen at any time and at any place. It can be a tailgate party at a 49'er game, a trip to the Napa Valley wine country, a day sailing on San Francisco Bay, a drive to the Santa Cruz beaches, or just to the backyard. Wherever your picnicing pleasure takes you, food always takes on new and exciting tastes when eaten outdoors.

This country picnic loaf is the answer to all your troubles. It can be served as an appetizer, a main course, or just handed out as sandwiches. In my picnic basket, I take along a variety of raw vegetables for munching with some garlic mayonnaise, a bottle of red or white wine and a batch of homemade brownies.

Bake this just before you leave on your trip. Keep it wrapped in foil until you are ready to serve it. (Several thickness of newspapers will keep it insulated for several hours.) Slice it immediately before you plan to enjoy it.

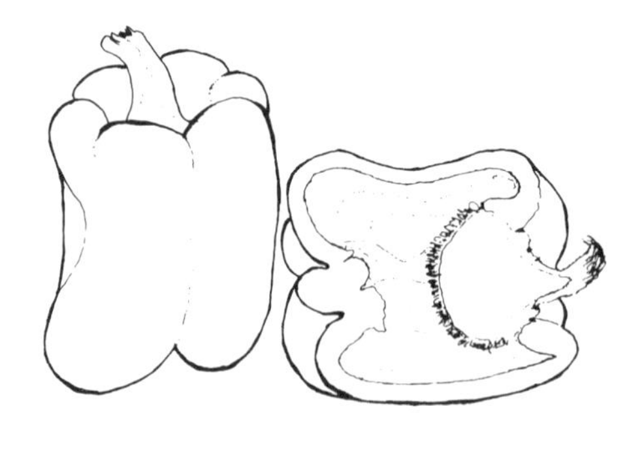

1 Loaf sourdough French bread, round
Butter, softened
4 Tablespoons olive oil
1 Small red onion, thinly sliced
5 Garlic cloves, finely chopped
½ Red bell pepper, coarsely chopped
½ Green bell pepper, coarsely chopped
1 Tablespoon butter
4 Ounces cooked ham, chopped
6 Eggs, beaten
1 Teaspoon curry powder
1 Teaspoon cayenne pepper
8 Slices Italian hard salami, diced
4 Ounces shrimp
Freshly ground pepper, to taste
8 Ounces grated cheese (Jack, Swiss or Cheddar)

Cut sourdough bread in half and scoop out enough bread on upper and lower sections with a sharp knife to form a dishlike loaf. Spread each section with some softened butter. Saute garlic, onions and peppers in olive oil until onions are transparent, approximately 5-7 minutes. Add pepper. In another skillet, saute ham with 1 tablespoon butter for 2-3 minutes. Add eggs. Cook over low heat. When eggs start to set, add salami and shrimp. Stir until all ingredients are hot. Cover the bottom loaf with garlic, onion and bell pepper mixture. Spoon egg mixture on top. Sprinkle with the grated cheese. Top with the remaining half loaf. Wrap tightly in foil and bake in a preheated 350° oven for 30 minutes. Slice in pie-shaped wedges and serve.

Kiwi Freezer Jam

Jams and jellies made from fresh fruit can be successfully frozen for 6-8 months. This kiwi jam will retain the fresh taste and clear color it attains just after preserving for many months. Any type of berries may be substituted. Adjust the sugar according to the sweetness of the fruit.

3 Cups peeled and mashed kiwi (about 10) at room temperature
¼ Cup lemon juice, freshly squeezed
3 Cups sugar
¾ Cup water
1 Package powdered fruit pectin (2 ounces)
Sterlized jars with tight-fitting lids, for freezing

In bowl, combine kiwi fruit, lemon juice and sugar. Stir to blend thoroughly; let stand 30 minutes. Meanwhile, mix water and pectin in a small saucepan. Bring to a full boil. Boil 1 minute, stirring constantly. Stir into kiwi mixture all at once. Continue stirring 3 minutes. Immediately ladle into the sterilized jars, leaving ½ inch space at the top of each jar. Wipe the rim with a clean, damp towel. Cover with lids. Let stand at room temperature 24 hours; then store in the freezer. (It will also keep in the refrigerator up to three weeks). This is not a firm jam, it should be a soft, spreadable consistency. Yield: about 7 cups.

Sweet Pepper Relish

This recipe for sweet pepper relish has been in our family for years. Mom prepares it during the summer canning season when both green and red peppers are abundant and low in price. It is a perfect accompaniment for hamburgers, hot dogs and it also makes a great salad dressing when combined with a few tablespoons of mayonnaise.

Safe canning requires proper containers, carefully prepared. The jars must be free of cracks and nicks to insure sealing. After cleaning both jars and lids, leave them in clean, hot water until immediately before you are ready to use them. Carefully remove the hot jars to a clean towel, fill at once and seal immediately.

2 Dozen sweet peppers (12 green, 12 red)
2 Large onions
3 Cups vinegar
3 Cups sugar
2 Tablespoons salt
2 Tablespoons mustard seed

Remove stems and seeds from peppers. Coarsely grind peppers and onions in a meat chopper or food processor. In a large kettle, combine peppers, onions, vinegar, sugar, salt and mustard seed. Boil 30 minutes. Pour into sterilized pint jars. Seal hot.

Peanut Brittle and Nut Crunch

My cousin, Kathleen O'Connor, gave me this quick and easy recipe for microwave peanut brittle. It is important that you have a candy thermometer so you'll know when the syrup reaches the hard crack stage. All microwaves have different cooking times which is why we allow the 4-6 minute variance.

The nut crunch is also easy, delicious and cooked in the microwave. Both candies will keep well when stored in an air tight container.

If you do not have a microwave, each candy can be prepared on top of the stove. Remember, however, the cooking times will be longer and the key is to cook the candies to the hard-crack stage, 290°F.

Peanut Brittle

2 Cups sugar
½ Cup light corn syrup
3 Tablespoons warm water
2 Tablespoons unsalted butter
1 Teaspoon vanilla
2 Cups roasted peanuts
1 Teaspoon baking soda

Lightly butter or grease a cookie sheet. Set aside. In a microwave proof 3 quart casserole, combine the sugar, corn syrup and water, stirring well to mix. Cook on high for 4-6 minutes, or until boiling. Stir. Cook on high an additional 4-6 minutes or until the syrup reaches 290°F, or the beginning of the hard-crack stage. When bubbling stops, stir in butter, vanilla, and nuts. Blend well. Stir in the soda (this will make a light, airy brittle). Pour immediately onto the lightly greased cookie sheet. Let cool for about 30 minutes and break into pieces.

Nut Crunch

1 Cup sugar
3 Tablespoons warm water
½ Cup unsalted butter
½ Cup roasted almonds, chopped (or walnuts or pecans)

Lightly butter or grease a cookie sheet. Set aside. In a microwave proof 3 quart casserole, combine the sugar and water; stir well. Add the butter. Cook on high for 3-4 minutes, or until boiling. Stir. Cook on high an additional 4-5 minutes or until the mixture almost reaches the hard-crack stage, 290°F. When bubbling stops, stir in the nuts. Pour onto the lightly buttered cookie sheet. Cool and break into pieces.

Seafood Dirty Rice

Seafood Dirty Rice is a creation of my friend, Paul Prudhomme, who is responsible for preserving and expanding the extraordinary Cajun and Creole cooking of Southern Louisiana.

Paul grew up south of Opelousas, Louisianna, in Acadian County. He spent twelve years in his own program of apprenticeship traveling throughout the country to work with chefs of every professional and ethnic background. In 1979, he and his wife opened their own restaurant, "K-Paul's Kitchen" which has been a smashing success ever since!

This dish would be a nice complement to a variety of entrees, but I prefer it with Paul's Blackened Redfish (page 134).

1 3/4 Pounds small shrimp with heads and shells
2 Tablespoons butter, unsalted
1 Tablespoon vegetable oil
1/2 Cup canned tomato sauce
3 Tablespoons onions, very finely chopped
2 1/2 Tablespoons green bell peppers, very finely chopped
2 Tablespoons celery, very finely chopped
1 Teaspoon garlic, minced
1 Teaspoon salt
1 Teaspoon white pepper
1 Teaspoon dried thyme leaves
1/2 Teaspoon ground red pepper (preferably cayenne)
1 1/2 Cups fish stock
1/2 Cup heavy cream
3 1/2 Cups cooked rice
3/4 Cup green onion, very finely chopped
1 Cup, packed lump crabmeat, about 1/2 pound

Peel the shrimp and use the heads and shells to make the fish stock; refrigerate shrimp until ready to use. In a large skillet, melt the butter with the oil. Add the tomato sauce, onions, bell peppers, celery, garlic, salt, white pepper, thyme and red pepper. Saute over medium heat 5 minutes, stirring frequently. Add the stock and continue cooking over high heat for 10 minutes, stirring occasionally. Stir in the cream and simmer about 4 minutes. Add the shrimp and simmer 3 minutes longer, stirring occasionally. Stir in the rice, green onions and crabmeat keeping the lumps of crabmeat intact as much as possible. Heat through and serve immediately.

Upside Down Garlic Bomb

This "Garlic Bomb" is a wonderful frittata that is perfect for a light evening meal or a mid-morning brunch.

Garlic has grown in gardens in most parts of the world since the beginning of recorded history. The earliest records reveal that it played a major part in the history of diet, folk medicine and in the beliefs and rituals of religions, either worshipped as a God or scorned as an associate of the devil.

Garlic, like onions, isn't exceptional in its nutritional content; its major benefit is adding flavor and excitement to the food it accompanies.

This recipe was an entry in the 1986 Gilroy Garlic Festival Cook-off. It was submitted by Paul La Combe from Paris, France.

4 Tablespoons butter
20-30 Garlic cloves, peeled
1 Cup chicken stock
3 Medium onions, coarsely chopped
1 Tablespoon basil, freshly chopped
1 Tablespoon parsley, freshly chopped
1 Teaspoon fresh rosemary (or ½ teaspoon dried)
6 Eggs
½ Cup heavy cream
½ Cup Parmesan cheese, freshly grated
½ Cup Swiss cheese, freshly grated
Freshly ground pepper, to taste

In a skillet, melt 1 tablespoon of butter. Add the garlic and slowly brown until edges are golden. Transfer garlic to a small oven proof baking dish and cover with chicken stock. Bake 1 hour at 375°. Add more stock or water if necessary. Garlic should not dry out. In a skillet over low heat, saute onions in remaining 3 tablespoons of butter. Add basil, parsley, rosemary and poached garlic to onion mixture. Add additional butter if mixture seems dry. Spread this garlic-onion mixture on the bottom of an oven proof skillet or dutch oven. In a separate bowl, combine the eggs, beaten until thick and frothy, heavy cream, Parmesan cheese, Swiss cheese and pepper. Pour the egg-cheese mixture slowly over the garlic-onion layer. Bake for 15 minutes at 450°. Reduce temperature to 350° and continue baking for additional 30 minutes. Check for doneness to your taste. If you prefer a firm, more set center, additional cooking may be required. Remove from oven. Let sit for a few minutes. Turn out the "Bomb" onto a preheated platter.

Yogurt Berry Pancakes

Barbara Lane, "People Are Talking's" restaurant critic, is the newest regular to join our staff. Once a month she appears with Ann and Ross to discuss the food, decor, service and prices in the Bay Area's restaurant scene. Her open approach is much admired and appreciated by our viewers.

When Barbara appeared as a guest chef, she brought with her a recipe for hotcakes from one of her favorite dining spots, "Campton Place," in San Francisco. This quietly luxurious small hotel dining room has become quite popular for its beautifully prepared, exquisite, delicious food. Chef Bradley Ogden, with his Mid-Western roots, has revitalized, with a simple, but sophisticated style, good American food. His dinners, as well as his breakfasts are a wonderful experience.

Mary and I cherish "Campton Place" as this is where we became engaged.

Honey Pecan Butter

⅓ Cup toasted pecans, finely chopped
½ Cup sweet butter, softened
¼ Cup honey

In a small bowl, beat the butter until smooth and soft. Beat in the honey. Add the chopped pecans and blend well. Cover and refrigerate. Let stand at room temperature to soften before serving.

1-1½ Pints strawberries, washed, hulled & quartered
2 Tablespoons sugar
½-⅔ Cup whole milk
9 Tablespoons butter, unsalted
1 Teaspoon vanilla extract
3 Cups cake flour
¼ Cup sugar
¾ Teaspoon baking soda
2 Tablespoons baking powder
1/8 Teaspoon salt
6 Large eggs
15 Ounces plain lowfat yogurt

Sprinkle strawberries with sugar. Let sit while preparing other ingredients. Combine milk and butter in a sauce pan and heat until butter melts. Remove from heat and add vanilla. Sift the dry ingredients into a large bowl. Whisk eggs in a separate bowl, just to blend. Add the warm milk/butter mixture to the eggs. Whisk again until combined. Add berries and their juice to the flour mixture. Mix to coat berries. Add the egg mixture to dry ingredients and fold. Mixture will look dry. Add yogurt and fold in. The batter will be quite thick and some lumps of flour will be noticeable. Do not overmix. If batter is too dry, add a little milk, but not more yogurt or pancakes will be too soft. Heat oiled griddle until a few drops of water 'skitter' across it. Use approximately ¼ cup batter for each hotcake. Turn when bubbles appear and pop. Cook until golden on each side. Serve at once with Honey Pecan Butter.

APPENDIX

"JOYCE JUE COOKING SCHOOL"
1980 Sutter, #303
San Francisco, California 94225

"GOURMET GUIDES"
1767 Stockton Street
San Francisco, California 94133
(415) 391-5903

"LITTLE JOE'S ITALIAN COOKBOOK"
Chronicle Books
One Hallidie Plaza
San Francisco, California 94102

"TURKEY DIET"
California Turkey Industry Board
P.O. Box 3329
Modesto, California 95353-3329
SEND $1.00 PER COPY

INDEX